A
CHEMICAL
FEAST

A CHEMICAL FEAST

By W. Harding leRiche

Facts On File Publications

New York, New York

A CHEMICAL FEAST

Library of Congress Cataloging in Publication Data

leRiche, W. Harding (William Harding), 1916-
  A Chemical feast.

  Includes index.
  1. Food. 2. Diet. 3. Diet in disease. I. Title.
TX353.L39   363.1'92   82-2442
ISBN 0-458-95420-9

PRINTED IN THE UNITED STATES OF AMERICA

987654321

FOR MARGARET

TABLE OF CONTENTS

Introduction and Acknowledgements

This book is a response to many questions that I have been asked by medical students, patients, and the general public during the last few years. *The Complete Family Book of Nutrition and Meal Planning* covered nutrition from a number of points of view, but it omitted several topics that are discussed in this book.

I wish to thank Mr. Fred Wardle of Methuen Publications for his interest and encouragement, and also Mr. William Minors and Mrs. Lesley Wiley for their help. Mr. Greg Cable saw the book through its final stages and our associates in the United States did the production very well. Marnie Collins, as always, was an accomplished editor. She trimmed the manuscript down to size and made it more readable.

W. Harding le Riche

Toronto, October 1982

A
CHEMICAL
FEAST

1.

Chemicals and the Normal Diet

There is today a great deal of misunderstanding about chemistry and the chemicals in our environment. Chemistry is simply the study of the composition of things. "Chemical" is not a four-letter word.

Consider this: You are perusing the supermarket shelves and come across a common product, honestly labeled as to its constituents. They include acetone, methyl acetate, furan, diacetyl, butanol, methyl furan, isoprene, methyl butanol, caffeine, essential oils, methanol, acetaldehyde, methyl formate, ethanol, dimethyl sulphide, and propionaldehyde. Would that make you nervous? You'd probably feel more comfortable if the product were simply labeled with its familiar name: Coffee.

The point is that everything is made up of chemicals. In fact, coffee is composed of at least 393, tea 188, cocoa 314. (Incidentally, even knowing all this, nobody has yet been able to synthesize good coffee, tea, or cocoa.) There is no need to be frightened of chemicals—they are everywhere, and relatively few of them have proven to be hazardous to human health.

Chemistry of the Human Body

The human body itself is a mass of chemicals, incredibly bound together in a complex way to make a functioning whole. Its complexity boggles the mind.

Table 1:1 shows the breakdown by weight of the basic elements in the body of a 160-pound (72 kg) man. Bear in mind that these are just the basic elements. These combine in different ways to form countless numbers of chemical substances. Perhaps the simplest example is the combination of hydrogen and oxygen—two of the predominant elements—to form water, H_2O, which in fact forms about two-thirds of the human body. Another example is hemoglobin, a highly complex and interesting chemical that enables oxygen from the air to be carried into the body. Other chemicals found in the blood include:

Acetone	Creatine
Albumin	Fatty Acids
Ammonia	Fibrinogen
Amylase	Globulin
Ascorbic Acid	Glucose
Bilirubin	Iodine
Calcium	Iron
Chloride	Lactic Acid
Cholesterol	and many many others.
Copper	

TABLE 1:1

THE ULTIMATE ELEMENTS IN THE BODY OF A MAN WEIGHING 160 POUNDS

Element	Pounds Weight in Body
Oxygen	104.0
Carbon	28.8
Hydrogen	16.0
Nitrogen	4.8
Calcium	2.4
Phosphorus	1.3
Potassium	0.6
Sulphur	0.4
Sodium	0.2
Chlorine	0.2

Small amounts of Magnesium, Iron, Manganese, Copper, Iodine, Cobalt, Fluorine, Zinc, Chromium, Molybdenum, Selenium.

Data recalculated from Hall, R. H. (1974) Food For Naught. The Decline in Nutrition. Harper and Row. Hagerstown.

We certainly don't know all the chemical combinations in the human body, but we do know a great deal about them. It is the fascinating science of the biochemist to find out exactly how the human body functions and how diseases can possibly be treated by modification of body chemistry.

A group of chemical substances in the body that are familiar to most people are the vitamins (Table 1:2), a group of organic compounds essential, though in small quantities, for the normal metabolism of other nutrients and the maintenance of overall well-being. These compounds can't be synthesized in the body; they must be obtained from the diet. They represent very different chemical compositions, and each has its own function in the body. Most foods contain several vitamins, but no one food contains all of them in sufficient quantity to satisfy human requirements under normal conditions.

TABLE 1:2

VITAMINS ESSENTIAL TO HUMAN NUTRITION

Original Name	Current Name
Vitamin A (anti-infective)	Vitamin A (retinol)
Vitamin B$_1$ (anti-beriberi; antineuritic)	Thiamine (Vitamin B$_1$)
Vitamin G (B$_2$)	Riboflavin
Pellagra preventive factor	Niacin (Nicotinic acid)
	Vitamin B$_6$ (Pyridoxine)
Vitamin B-complex	
	Vitamin B$_{12}$ (cyanocobalamin)
	Folacin (Folic acid Pteroylglutamic acid)
	Pantothenic acid
	Biotin
Vitamin C	Ascorbic acid
Vitamin D	Vitamin D (calciferol)
Vitamin E	Vitamin E (alpha-tocopherol)
Vitamin K	Vitamin K (menaquinone, and phylloquinones)

We mention vitamins specifically in our discussion of chemicals because many people feel there is a difference between "natural vitamins" and "chemical vitamins." There is none whatsoever. Natural vitamin C, as found in orange juice and cabbage, and chemical vitamin C, as synthesized in the laboratory, are identical. The chemical formula of vitamin C is the same, whether it comes from an orange or a pill.

Chemicals Added to Foods

Chemical additives are nothing new. They have been used since civilization began. Some of the earliest were preservatives— salt, sodium nitrate, sugar, vinegar, and smoke. All of these limit or stop bacterial growth. In the "good old days," food was foul. Even when preservatives were used, the chemicals were not necessarily pure, nor were their effects generally understood. Furthermore, until the development of pesticides, many foods were contaminated by insects, fungi, and bacteria. The first general food law was the Netherlands Law of 1829, followed by the British Pure Food Law of 1860. Neither completely remedied the problem of irresponsible food adulteration, but consider:

In the 18th century vinegar was often dilute sulfuric acid, while copper salts were used to improve the color of green vegetables. In England in 1751, some types of gin included the following:

oil of vitriol (sulfuric acid)
oil of almonds
oil of turpentine
spirits of wine
lump sugar
lime water
rose water
alum
salt of tartar (presumably potassium hydrogen tartrate)
Obviously a very powerful drink!

Foods today in North America are cleaner than they have ever been. As a result of careful checking by governmental agencies, and barring accidents, foods are not poisonous, even if they have been treated with pesticides, as we shall see in a later chapter. Additives are used only for specific purposes, and they, too, are discussed in a subsequent chapter.

In general, I would personally prefer to eat foods that have been as little modified as possible, but I know that in some instances foods must be modified, physically or chemically, in order to preserve them or add to their palatability.

The Human Diet

One of the keys to the survival of the human race is that human beings will eat almost anything. Table 1:3 represents a list of the foods people eat around the world. We are truly omnivorous.

TABLE 1:3

A LIST OF HUMAN FOODSTUFFS

A. Animal Products	B. Plant Products
1. *Milk:* Cow, water buffalo, goat, sheep, camel, horse, reindeer, caribou, yak.	1. *Grains* (cereals): Wheat, rice, corn (maize). sorghum, millet, buckwheat, rye, barley, oats.
2. *Meat and entrails (liver, tripe, sweetbreads, blood):* Beef, mutton, pork, veal, goat, reindeer, camel, rabbit, horse, dog, yak.	2. *Pulses:* Beans of all types, peas, lentils, broadbeans, cowpeas, vetch (fitch).
3. *Game and venison:* Deer, moose, elk, antelope, caribou, hare, hippopotamus, monkey, polar bear.	3. *Fruits* (a) Tropical: Banana, plantain, pineapple, papaya (paw paw), avocado, mango, guava, passion fruit, bread fruit, loquat.
4. *Poultry* (a) *Domesticated Fowl:* Chicken, turkey, duck, goose, pigeon, pheasant, guineahen. (b) *Wild Fowl:* Grouse, partridge,	(b) Subtropical: Orange, lemon, grapefruit, tangerine, lime, citron, figs, pomegranate, persimmon, cactus fruits.

TABLE 1:3 (continued)

A LIST OF HUMAN FOODSTUFFS

A. Animal Products	B. Plant Products
quail, pheasant, ptarmigan, duck, goose, pigeon.	(c) Deciduous fruits: Apple, pear, grape, quince.
(c) *Miscellaneous:* e.g., swallow's nest	(d) Stone fruits: Cherry, peach, nectarine, apricot, plum.
5. *Eggs:* A great variety: Chicken, duck, goose, ostrich, penguin.	(e) Berries: Strawberries, raspberries, blackberries, boysenberries, cloudberries, cranberries, elderberries, black currants, gooseberries, red currants.
6. *Fish* (Flesh, liver, roe): (a) Saltwater: Herring, sardine, tuna, mackerel, salmon, cod, haddock, ocean perch, plaice, sole, dolphin, swordfish, shark, dogfish.	
(b) Freshwater: (i) Wild. Pike, perch, whitefish, loach, trout, salmon, sturgeon, bass, pickerel. (ii) Cultivated. Carp, eel, tench, catfish, tilapia.	4. *Melons and Squashes:* Cantaloupe, honey dew, watermelon and other melons, squashes, pumpkins, cucumbers.
7. *Shellfish* (a) Crustacean: Crabs, lobsters, crayfish, crawfish, shrimp, prawns.	5. *Vegetables:* (a) Leafy: Cabbage, spinach, brussels sprouts, artichoke, leeks, lettuce, endive, bamboo shoots, palm hearts, various herbs.
(b) Molluscs: Oyster, mussel, scallop, squid, octopus, snails (escargots).	(b) Root Vegetables: Carrots, parsnip, turnip, rutabaga, radish, beet.
8. *Miscellaneous* Frogs' legs, snakes, turtles, terrapin,	(c) Seeds: Green peas, green beans, lima beans, okra. (d) Others:

TABLE 1:3 (continued)

A LIST OF HUMAN FOODSTUFFS

A. Animal Products	B. Plant Products
insects (locusts, flying ants, beetles, grubs), sea cucumbers.	Cauliflower, broccoli, onions, garlic, tomatoes.

6. *Tubers:* Irish or white potatoes, sweet potatoes (yams), taro, cassava, Jerusalem artichoke, true yams.
7. *Nuts:* Almond, Brazil nut, cashew, breadnut, butternut, chestnut, filbert, peanut (groundnut), pecan, pistachio, walnut.
8. *Fungi:* Various yeasts, bakers', brewers', food yeast. Various types of mushrooms.
9. *Honey*
10. *Sugar:* Sugar cane, sugar beet, maple syrup, date palm sugar.
11. *Oil seeds:* Soya, olive, peanut, sunflower, safflower, cottonseed, rapeseed, palm kernels, sesame seeds.
12. *Seaweed:* Various types.
13. *Beverages:* Tea, coffee, cocoa, mint, yerba maté.
14. *Alcoholic Beverages:* A wide variety. This immense list illustrates that people in their urge for survival will eat almost anything.

After a great deal of study, and a certain amount of educated guesswork, most countries of the world began establishing food guides, recommending the types and amounts of foods to be eaten daily to obtain the necessary quantities of basic nutrients. The U.S. and Canadian guides are shown in Tables 1:4 and 1:5.

TABLE 1:4

DAILY FOOD GUIDE—THE BASIC FOUR FOOD GROUPS

Food Group	Main Nutrients	Daily Amounts
Milk Milk, cheese, ice cream, or other products made with whole or skimmed milk	Calcium Protein Riboflavin	Children under 9 2 or 3 cups. Children 9 to 12 3 or more cups Teenagers 4 or more cups Pregnant women 3 or more cups. Nursing mothers 4 or more cups. (1 cup = 8 oz. fluid milk or designated milk equivalent†)
Meats Beef, veal, lamb, pork, poultry, fish, eggs	Protein Iron Thiamine	2 or more servings Count as one serving 2 or 3 oz. of lean, boneless meat, poultry, or fish
Alternates Dry beans, dry peas, nuts, peanut butter	Niacin	2 eggs 1 cup cooked dry beans or peas 4 tablespoons peanut butter
Vegetables and fruits		4 or more servings Count as 1 serving ½ cup of vegetable or fruit, or a portion such as 1 medium

TABLE 1:4 (continued)

DAILY FOOD GUIDE—THE BASIC FOUR FOOD GROUPS

Food Group	Main Nutrients	Daily Amounts
	Vitamin A	apple, banana, orange, potato, or ½ a medium grapefruit, melon. Include A dark-green or deep-yellow vegetable or fruit rich in Vitamin A, at least every other day
	Vitamin C (ascorbic acid) Smaller amounts of other vitamins and minerals	A citrus fruit or other fruit or vegetable rich in vitamin C Daily Other vegetables and fruits including potatoes
Breads and cereals	Thiamine Niacin Riboflavin Iron Protein	4 or more servings of whole grain. Count as 1 serving 1 slice of bread 1 ounce (1 cup) ready to eat cereal, flake or puff varieties ½ to ¾ cup cooked cereal ½ to ¾ cup cooked pasta (macaroni, spaghetti, noodles) Crackers 5 saltines, 2 squares graham crackers, etc.

*Use additional amounts of these foods or added butter, margarine, oils, sugars, etc., as desired or needed.

†Milk equivalents: 1 ounce cheddar cheese, 3 servings cottage cheese, 1 cup fluid skimmed milk, 1 cup buttermilk, ¼ cup dry skimmed milk powder, 1 cup ice milk. 1⅔ cups ice cream, ½ cup evaporated milk.

Source: Williams, S. R. (1973) *Nutrition and Diet Therapy.* C.V. Mosby Company, St. Louis.

TABLE 1:5

CANADA'S FOOD GUIDE

These foods are good to eat. Eat them every day for health.
Have three meals each day.

Milk Children (up to about
  11 years ...... 2½ cups   Whole, 2%, skim, or
              (20 fl. oz.)   powdered milk, cheese,
Adolescents 4   cups   ice cream; or soups made
              (32 fl. oz.)   with milk all supply
Adults ... 1½ cups (12 fl. necessary calcium,
                      oz.)   riboflavin, and protein.
Expectant and
  nursing mothers .. 4
      cups (32 fl. oz.)

Fruit Two servings of fruit   Selections could be fresh
or juice, including a   or canned fruits
satisfactory source of   (grapefruit, peaches, dried
vitamin C (ascorbic acid)   fruits (prunes, raisins), or
such as oranges, tomatoes,   fruit juices (tomato,
and vitaminized apple   orange). Most fruits are
juice.   sources of vitamin C,
                                 vitamin A, and iron.

Vegetables One serving of   Raw, cooked, frozen, or
potatoes. Two servings of   canned vegetables such as
other vegetables,   cabbage, broccoli, carrots,
preferably yellow or green   peas, turnips, and potato
and often raw.   provide vitamin C, vitamin
                               A, folic acid, and iron.

Bread and cereals Bread   Whole-grain breads and
(with butter or fortified   cereals and enriched
margarine). One serving   products (breads, cereals,
of whole grain cereal.   macaroni, spaghetti)
                               supply thiamine,
                               riboflavin, niacin, and
                               iron.

Meat and fish One serving   Foods such as hamburger,
of meat, fish, or poultry.   fish chowder, baked beans,

TABLE 1:5 (continued)

CANADA'S FOOD GUIDE

These foods are good to eat. Eat them every day for health.
Have three meals each day.

Eat liver occasionally. Eggs, cheese, dried beans or peas may be used in place of meat. In addition, eggs and cheese at least three times a week.	cheese omelets, and peanut butter also contain valuable protein, iron, B vitamins, and Vitamin A.
Vitamin D 400 International Units, for all growing persons and expectant and nursing mothers.	Sources of vitamin D include vitamin D-fortified milk and margarine, cod liver oil, or a vitamin D supplement.

The main food elements are carbohydrates or starches, proteins, fats, minerals, vitamins, water, and fiber or roughage.

In the carbohydrate group are various sugars and starches. Sucrose, which is cane or beet sugar, has become a favored item of diet in modern times, and in fact many people feel that we eat far too much of it. It provides about one quarter of the total carbohydrate in our diet. Starch is a more complex compound composed of many glucose chains. The major sources of starch are the food grains, sweet potatoes, potatoes, fruit, vegetables, and legumes. In tropical countries sources of starch include yams, bananas, cassava, taro, sago, and others. Cooking starch not only improves the flavor; it also breaks down and softens the starch cells.

Another carbohydrate is cellulose, which forms the fiber in plants. Although ruminants, such as cattle, sheep, and goats, can digest it, humans can't. But for this very reason, cellulose adds bulk to the diet, and it is of considerable importance in the prevention of constipation.

Proteins are the basic structural components of every living cell. Proteins are built up of amino acids, of which there are 22. Thirteen of them can be manufactured by the body and thus are known as "non-essential." The other nine—the essential amino acids—must be obtained in our diet. Proteins containing all nine essential amino acids are known as "complete" proteins.

Although most of us think "meat" when we think of protein, plant foods are important sources. Indeed, as animal proteins become more expensive to produce, we will have to do more research into plant proteins. We need to know much more about the various combinations possible from plant proteins that will build up proteins adequate for human growth. For example, although the protein in corn is not complete, it can be improved to the value of skimmed milk by adding to it the amino acids tryptophan, lysine, and isoleucine. Wheat flour

TABLE 1:6

PROTEIN CONTENT OF COMMON FOODS

Edible Food Substances	Kcal per 100 Grams	Grams of Protein per 100 Grams
Pork meat, medium fat (cooked)	457	14.9
Beef meat, medium fat (cooked)	273	17.5
Chicken meat (total edible)	302	18.0
Fish fillet (unspecified)	132	18.8
Canned tuna (low fat)	128	28.3
Canned tuna oil	217	27.7
Pacific sardines (canned in tomatoes)	216	17.8
Salmon, canned	173	20.2
Eggs, fresh	144	11.0
Eggs, dehydrated	605	47.0
Milk, whole	68	3.5
Skim milk, dry	360	36.0
Cheese, hard	341	34.0
Rice	360	6.7
Corn	356	9.3
Wheat flour (medium extraction)	350	11.7
Potatoes	70	1.7
Soybean grits	261	46.0
Beans, peas, dry	345	22.2

can be markedly improved by the addition of lysine and threonine. The day might well come when this type of procedure will be carried out on a large scale.

In the average western European and North American diet we eat a very high proportion of fats and oils, something in the order of 35 to 40 per cent of our total calories. On the other hand, most of the people of South America, Asia, and Africa eat very little fat. The relationship of fats to heart disease is an interesting one, and one that we'll look at in a later chapter.

We've already touched on vitamins. The most important point to remember about them is this: In a good mixed diet, most people will find enough vitamins for their needs. The exception is that infants and young children may need added vitamins A and D. Pure vitamin deficiencies—deficiencies in one vitamin only—are rare, with the exception of vitamin D deficiency, which produces rickets, or scurvy, resulting from a lack of vitamin C, conditions sometimes found in children. Much more common is general malnutrition—vitamin deficiencies as well as deficiency in protein. Malnutrition exists in North America, and it is widespread in the Third World.

Dietary Standards Around the World

It is usually assumed that the dietary standards set by various agencies are immutable, that they must be followed to the letter. This is not the case. Not only do diet patterns and food values vary from place to place, but specific requirements for particular nutrients may also vary, depending upon environmental factors, the genetic background of the people concerned, the particular diet patterns, the nature of stress situations, and the age, sex, and rate of growth of the people concerned. It is not possible to devise a general diet plan suitable for every single person. The best we can do is to lay down standards that are generally adequate and satisfactory. In North America, we seem to have developed dietary standards that make for maximum size, early maturity, active sex life, and maximum muscular development. Whether all these qualities are necessarily important for a long and healthy life is open to question.

It should be very clearly understood that the recommen-

dations of scientific bodies on dietary standards cannot be used
to determine the state of nutrition of individuals. In other words,
it is misguided to compare diets with a standard and then to
conclude that the people who do not reach the standard are
malnourished. The diagnosis of malnutrition is essentially a
clinical and biochemical determination based on the examination of *individuals*. Food intake influences physical condition
only if it is markedly deficient, either in total amount or in
quality.

Dietary standards have three practical uses.
1. In the planning of food production and distribution processes;
2. In the planning of mass feeding or food-rationing;
3. As a reasonable starting point for nutritional therapy.
Bearing this in mind, it's interesting to compare the U.S.,
Canadian, and Japanese standards (Table 1:7). The United States
National Research Council has decided that the protein allowance at the time this table was made was 0.928 g/kg of body
weight, which amounts to 65 g per day for the average 70 kg
man. In actual fact this amount of protein is probably twice
what is really needed. The Canadian scientists using the same
data concluded that the protein requirement for a 70 kg adult
male is approximately 47 g per day, or about 72 per cent of the
recommendations of the National Research Council in the United
States. This considerable difference indicates the widely varying interpretations that can be placed on the same scientific
data.

Calcium is another bone of contention (no pun intended).
The Food and Agricultural Organization and World Health
Organization decided that intakes of 400 to 500 mg per day of
calcium represented a practical allowance for adults. The
Canadian recommendations are close to this, but the American
standards are higher—800 mg. We suspect that this standard
is influenced far more by dietary preferences in the United
States than by scientific proof. It has been pointed out by
Professor Mark Hegsted, an eminent authority on nutrition,
that although most people of the world do not consume enough
calcium to meet dietary recommendations, there is no convincing evidence that they are deficient. The Chinese, in particular,
have always consumed much less calcium than is usually

TABLE 1:7

UNITED STATES, CANADIAN AND JAPANESE RECOMMENDED DIETARY INTAKES FOR YOUNG, HEALTHY, NORMALLY ACTIVE, MALE ADULTS**

Standard	Wt. in lbs.	Calories	Protein gm	Calcium gm	Vitamin A-I.U.	Iron mg	Thiamin mg	Riboflavin mg	Niacin mg	Ascorbic Acid-mg	Vitamin D-I.U.
National Research Council United States	154	2800	65	0.8	5000*	10	1.4	1.7	18 (equiv.)	60	0
Dietary Standard for Canada	158	2850	48	0.5	3700†	6	0.9	1.4	9	30	0
Standard Nutritional Requirements for Japanese (light work)	123	2500	70	0.6	2000‡	10	1.3	1.3	13	65	400

*Assuming two-thirds of the total vitamin A activity as carotene and one-third as the preformed vitamin. If the sole
source of vitamin A.

†Based on the mixed Canadian diet supplying both vitamin A and carotene. As the preformed vitamin A, the suggested intake would be about two-thirds of that indicated.

‡All as preformed vitamin A.

**The figures given in this table, and elsewhere in this chapter for agency-recommended dietary intakes are those which were current at the time of revision of this chapter (March 1972). The Food and Nutrition Board of the National Research Council, in common with the other mentioned agencies, periodically revises its recommendations, a fact which emphasizes, of course, the tentative nature of the recommendations.

Source: Goodhart, R. S. (1973) Criteria of an Adequate Diet. from Goodhart, R. S. and Shils, M. E. (1973). Modern Nutrition in Health and Disease. Fifth Edition. Lea and Febiger, Philadelphia.

recommended, yet their teeth develop normally and their skeletons hold together perfectly well.

Real calcium deficiency has recently been described by Dr. John Pettifor of Johannesburg, South Africa. However, we feel that nutritionists who advocate enormous intakes of milk because milk provides calcium should reconsider their position. The older dietary standards set by the Japanese set high calcium intake levels. This seems to be more of a political than a scientific decision, because the Japanese wanted to develop bigger people. However, they have now somewhat reduced their recommendations for calcium intake. There is no doubt that Japanese who grow up in North America tend to be larger than their parents, and also larger than people in Japan. So, no doubt, food intake in general, particularly intake of protein and possibly calcium, does have an influence on the final size people may reach. But there's no guarantee that large people are healthier than small people.

Both the U.S. and Canadian recommendations are in excess of known minimal requirements, and in some instances, of course, the standards are approximations. The standards are quite adequate for the purposes, mentioned previously, for which they were designed. However, there is no evidence that eating more of the dietary elements than are shown in the standards will be of added benefit to health. As a matter of fact, if people eat much more than the standard suggests, they may grow fat, which is definitely not to be recommended.

In Table 1:8 we can see some interesting changes in U.S. dietary standards over a 10-year period. Recommended protein intakes in females aged 19 to 22 were reduced from 55 to 44 g, vitamin A requirements from 1000 mcg to 800, Vitamin D from 10 mcg to 7.5, vitamin E from 25 to 8 mg, and vitamin B_{12} from 5 to 3 mcg. There was also a reduction in magnesium from 350 to 300 mg and slight increases in niacin, from 13 to 14 mg, and iodine, from 100 to 150 mcg.

Obviously, then, dietary requirements are not static. They change as opinions change and as knowledge increases. Dietary standards are not true for all time. That is why people who teach nutrition should continuously update their knowledge; otherwise they might find themselves preaching the wrong gospel!

TABLE 1:8

A TEN-YEAR HISTORY OF RECOMMENDED DAILY DIETARY ALLOWANCES 1968-79. FOOD AND NUTRITION BOARD, NATIONAL ACADEMY OF SCIENCES—NATIONAL RESEARCH COUNCIL, U.S.A., FEMALE 19-22 (A)

Fat-Soluble Vitamins

Weight kg. lbs.	Height cm. in.	Year	Protein grams	Vitamin A micrograms R.E. (b)	Vitamin D micrograms (c)	Vitamin E mg. αTE (d)
58 128	163 64	1968	55	1000	10	25
58 128	162 65	1973	46	800	10	12
55 120	163 64	1979	44	800	7.5	8

Water-Soluble Vitamins

Years	Vitamin C mg.	Folacin (f) micrograms	Niacin mg. N.E. (e)	Riboflavin mg.	Thiamin mg.	Vitamin B₆ mg.	Vitamin B₁₂ micrograms (g)
1968	55	400	13	1.5	1.0	2.0	5
1973	45	400	14	1.4	1.1	2.0	3.0
1979	60	400	14	1.3	1.1	2.0	3.0

Minerals

Year	Calcium mg.	Phosphorus mg.	Iodine micrograms	Iron mg.	Magnesium mg.	Zinc mg.
1968	800	800	100	18	350	—
1973	800	800	100	18	300	15
1979	800	800	150	18	300	15

(a) The allowances are intended to provide for individual variations among most normal persons as they live in the United States under usual environmental stresses. Diets should be based on a variety of common foods in order to provide other nutrients for which human requirements have been less well defined.

(b) Retinol equivalents   1 Retinol equivalent
                                 = 1 microgram retinol or 6 micrograms carotene

(c) As cholecalciferol: 10 micrograms cholecalciferol = 400 I.U. Vitamin D

(d) α (alpha) tocopherol equivalents 1 mg d-α-tocopherol = 1αTE

(e) 1 N.E. (niacin equivalent) is equal to 1 mg. of niacin or 60 mg. of dietary tryptophan

TABLE 1:8 (continued)

A TEN-YEAR HISTORY OF RECOMMENDED DAILY DIETARY ALLOWANCES 1968–79. FOOD AND NUTRITION BOARD, NATIONAL ACADEMY OF SCIENCES—NATIONAL RESEARCH COUNCIL, U.S.A., FEMALE 19–22 (A)

(f) The folacin allowances refer to dietary sources as determined by Lactobacillus casei assay after treatment with enzymes ("conjugases") to make polyglutamyl forms of the vitamin available to the test organism.

(g) The RDA for Vitamin B_{12} in infants is based on average concentration of the vitamins in human milk. The allowances after weaning are based on energy intake (as recommended by the American Academy of Pediatrics) and considerations of other factors such as intestinal absorption.

These tables are quoted from "The Recommended Dietary Allowances." *Nutrition Today* 1979, 14:10–14.

Diet Fads

During recent years there has been a development of what amounts to a mythology in connection with diet modification. It has been claimed, for instance, by Senator McGovern of the United States, that if the dietary goals recommended by his Select Committee were adopted, dying from cancer would be reduced by 20 per cent, death from heart disease by 25 per cent, and tooth decay would become a thing of the past. If only this were true!

The originators of the dietary fiber hypothesis promise to reduce morbidity and mortality in a number of areas of disease, including atheroma, appendicitis, constipation, cancer of the colon, coronary thrombosis, dental caries, deep vein thrombosis, diabetes mellitus, gallstones, diverticulitis, hiatus hernia, hemorrhoids, peptic ulcer, polyps of the bowel, and varicose veins. Some widespread benefits have also been assumed following a fall in sucrose or salt consumption.

Each of these faiths has a band of loyal followers who have been promoting their ideas with evangelical zeal. The unfortunate part about these ideas is that, while some are strongly suggestive, most are not fully proven. There is certainly evidence that diet can do good to people, but there is only limited evidence that miracles can be brought about by dietary manipulation. For example, there *is* evidence that deaths from ischemic heart disease may be related to diet, for the most part evidence of an epidemiological nature based on large-scale statistical correlation studies. But proof of the hypothesis requires detailed, controlled clinical experimentation, some of which is currently being done. The final answers are not yet with us, and they may never be complete, because it is daily becoming more improbable that we can carry out large, well-planned human experiments. What will stop the human experiments will be the cost.

2.
Dietary Changes and Malnutrition in North America

People live longer than they used to. In 1900, the average baby born could expect to live 49.24 years; by 1977, the average expectation of life in the United States was 73.2 years. Part of the reason is improved diet, as we shall see. But a large part is due to the striking decrease in deaths from infectious diseases. Nowadays more people in the western world are dying of ischemic heart disease, cancer, or other metabolic diseases that are apparently related to diet and the general way of life.

Certain interesting changes have taken place in the average North American diet between 1900 and 1974. As Table 2:1 shows, most people consumed about the same number of calories daily (food energy), but fewer of them came from carbohydrates. Protein consumption stayed about the same, but an ever-increasing proportion of it came fron animal sources— people have been eating more meat and dairy products, fewer cereals. Fat consumption increased, and we can see from Table 2:2 that the proportion of unsaturated fats has increased much more than that of saturated fats. The amount of fiber in the average diet has steadily decreased, perhaps as a result of the decrease in cereal consumption.

As for minerals (Table 2:3), while calcium and iron intake increased slightly, phosphorus consumption remained fairly

TABLE 2:1

NUTRIENTS CONTRIBUTING FOOD ENERGY AVAILABLE FOR CONSUMPTION PER PERSON PER DAY 1909–1974, U.S.A.

Year	Food Energy Kilograms	Carbo- hydrate grams	Total grams	Animal grams	Vege- table grams	Fat grams
1909	3530	497	104	54	50	127
1919	3440	478	97	52	45	130
1929	3460	471	94	51	43	137
1939	3340	439	92	53	39	139
1949	3200	399	94	60	34	140
1959	3170	376	95	64	31	147
1969	3280	381	100	69	31	154
1974	3350	388	101	70	31	154

(Protein = Total grams, Animal grams, Vege-table grams)

Source: Gortner, W. A. (1975) Nutrition in The United States, 1900 to 1974. Cancer Research 35:3246–3253

TABLE 2:2

CRUDE FIBER AND FOOD LIPIDS AVAILABLE PER PERSON PER DAY IN THE U.S.A. FOOD SUPPLY

Years	Total Nutrient Fat	Fatty Acids Saturated Grams	Oleic Acid Grams	Linoleic Acid Grams	Cholesterol milligrams	Crude Fiber Grams
1909– 1913	125	50.3	51.5	10.7	509	6.1
1935– 1939	133	52.9	54.4	12.7	493	5.5
1957– 1959	143	54.7	58.2	16.6	578	4.4
1970	157	55.9	63.1	23.3	556	4.2
1974	158	56.0	62.9	24.2		4.3

Source: Gortner, W. A. (1975) Cancer Research, 35:3246–3253.

TABLE 2:3

MINERAL NUTRIENTS AVAILABLE FOR
CONSUMPTION PER PERSON PER DAY 1909–1974

Year	Calcium grams	Phosphorus grams	Iron milligrams	Magnesium milligrams
1909	0.83	1.58	15.5	
1919	0.84	1.51	15.1	
1929	0.88	1.51	14.3	
1939	0.91	1.48	14.0	·
1949	0.98	1.52	16.4	
1959	0.98	1.52	16.2	
1969	0.94	1.53	17.6	
1974	0.95	1.54	18.3	348

Source: Gortner, W. A. (1975) Cancer Research 35:3246–3253.

constant. Table 2:4 demonstrates that the average person's vitamin intake has been slowly but steadily increasing.

What all this means in real terms is that, in addition to
eating more meat, especially poultry, people are also eating
more fruits and vegetables. Both potatoes and eggs have suffered
a decline in popularity, perhaps because of bad, and not especially well-founded, publicity.

So the average North American is eating better than ever
before. But "average" isn't everyone, and "better" doesn't
mean ideally. People in depressed economic areas have always
had, and still have, bad diets. And there are many poor people
in North America.

Nutritional Deficiency Diseases

Fortunately, deaths from diseases like pellagra are largely a
thing of the past. Pellagra, the result of a lack of complete
protein in the diet, was widespread in the southern U.S. during
the 1920s and 1930s, when many people subsisted on corn. At
the same time, scurvy, from vitamin C deficiency, was not

TABLE 2:4

VITAMIN NUTRIENTS AVAILABLE FOR
CONSUMPTION PER PERSON PER DAY 1909–1974

Year	Vitamin A I.U.	Thiamin milli- grams	Riboflavin milli- grams	Niacin milli- grams	Ascorbic Acid mil.	Vitamin B_6 milli- grams	Vitamin B_{12} micro- grams
1909	7,800	1.68	1.88	9.5	105		
1919	8,000	1.55	1.83	18.5	100		
1929	8,300	1.57	1.86	17.9	111		
1939	8,600	1.50	1.87	17.3	116		
1949	8,500	1.89	2.25	20.8	109		
1959	8,100	1.88	2.29	20.8	106		
1969	8,100	1.93	2.35	22.8	111		
1974	8,200	1.94	2.33	23.4	119	2.28	9.7

Source: Gortner, W. A. (1975) Cancer Research 35:3246–3253.

uncommon, and there were also cases of beriberi resulting from a deficiency of thiamin. Deficiency of vitamin A produced xerophthalmia; lack of vitamin D resulted in rickets. Knowledge of the causes of these conditions has largely eradicated them in North America, although serious deficiency diseases are again appearing among extremist vegetarian cults, particularly in small children.

Malnutrition

Between 1947 and 1958 in the United States, a number of nutritional surveys were carried out, comparing people's diets with the standards generally recommended. It was found that most people consumed less vitamin A, ascorbic acid, and iron than was believed to be necessary.

The problem with this kind of study is that it is open to a number of different interpretations. If an individual's diet doesn't exceed or equal a standard, it doesn't necessarily mean he or she is malnourished. Even a doctor's examination is not always a sure-fire method of determining the presence of malnutrition—all physicians do not agree on what constitutes malnutrition. Biochemical measurements, combined with clinical examination, are the only completely accurate way to determine an individual's nutritional state, and we need to use these methods to do further study of the nutritional standards themselves.

If we bear in mind, then, the weakness inherent in past studies, we can still draw some interesting conclusions. The first is that poor people do not eat as well as the rest of the population, which should come as no surprise. The children with the highest nutritional risk were pre-schoolers in the lower socio-economic groups, who appeared to have insufficient food, rather than food of inferior quality.

It is interesting to note that many pre-school children whose diets were more than adequate were also given vitamin supplements. In fact, many North Americans, adults as well as children, are taking unnecessarily high amounts of vitamins.

A 1968 survey studied the poorer areas in 10 states: Texas, Louisiana, Kentucky, Washington, Michigan, New York, West Virginia, California, South Carolina, and Massachusetts. In the areas surveyed, 55 per cent of the families were either in poverty or very close to it, with an income of less than $3000 per year. Nutritional standards generally were found to be inadequate, and obesity was common—in some groups over 50 per cent of adult women were obese. Iron-deficiency anemia was also common. Mexican Americans in particular seemed to have diets deficient in vitamin A.

Although this 10-state survey did not represent the total population of the United States, it did shatter some myths. Serious malnourishment existed in the best-fed country in the world. Dr. Arnold E. Schaefer, in charge of the project, concluded that 35 to 55 per cent of the people studied suffered from one or more nutrient deficiencies. Fifteen per cent of school children showed some growth retardation; one third had anemia to a degree that would require therapy. One third of the children suffered from vitamin A deficiency, and 4 per cent showed evidence of rickets. Four or 5 per cent had pot bellies, symptomatic of protein and calorie malnutrition.

A very surprising discovery was that 5 per cent of all people studied had an enlarged thyroid—that is, goiter—due to a low iodine intake. Goiter was thought to have been eradicated many years previously with the widespread use of iodized table salt. The truth is that iodization of salt is not compulsory all over the United States, and in many parts of the country untreated salt is widely used.

Dr. Schaefer inferred from this survey that at least 10 million Americans were markedly malnourished. We don't know if this figure is accurate, but certainly malnutrition does exist, and it is far from uncommon.

One of the greatest factors contributing to this state of affairs was and is lack of education. People do not know what foods to buy to get maximum nutrition for their food dollar. Complicating the problem is that food fortification is by no means universal. In the United States anyone can sell bread that is not enriched, milk that contains little or no vitamin A or D, salt that is not iodized. Many people don't know the difference or assume that all these products *are* fortified. Sadly, at one point the U.S. government was sending to undernourished people overseas products superior to those given to the native poor. For example, in 1965 the milk powder sent overseas was fortified with vitamins A and D. It was three years after this that milk powder distributed to the American poor was so fortified.

One of the survey's discoveries was that many children went to school without breakfast. This is, in fact, a common phenomenon, not just confined to the poor. Particularly in homes where both parents work, children are left to fend for themselves nutritionally, and they haven't the judgment to choose the right foods. They will inevitably choose things that taste good to them, without regard for nutritional values.

A recent Canadian survey showed that, although obvious malnutrition was not common, overweight was a great problem. Some iron deficiency was found, and the diets of many girls and pregnant women had inadequate calcium and vitamin D, although not sufficiently lacking to cause rickets. Native peoples displayed modest deficiencies of calcium and vitamins A and C. Increasing malnutrition is being found among the elderly all over North America as the cost of food rises.

The lesson in all this is that we need to be aware of the ever-present threat of malnutrition, even in our well-fed society, the more so as food and energy prices rise. With education and concerted effort, we can drastically reduce malnutrition in those groups of people hardest hit—the poor, the children, the elderly.

Obesity

A lot of North Americans are *over*nourished—obesity is becoming a widespread and serious health risk. As most people know, there is a definite correlation between overweight and the development of atherosclerosis and ischemic heart disease.

What is not clear is the relationship between fat and cholesterol intake and these same diseases. At one point nutritionists were convinced that lowering the consumption of saturated fat and cholesterol would perforce decrease the accumulation of cholesterol in the blood and thus decrease the chances of atherosclerosis and ischemic heart disease. But as more information accumulates, we are becoming less certain. It might well be that overall caloric intake may be as important a factor in these diseases as is fat consumption. The evidence is clear, though, that obesity is generally unhealthy.

Exercise

For most people in the western world, exercise is a rare event. It's encouraging, though, to see a growing awareness of the importance of physical fitness and a trend towards regular exercise. After millennia of intense physical activity in order just to survive, it's unlikely that the human animal could now be healthy while sitting on its collective butt.

Teenage Diets

One of the greatest problems amongst teenage North Americans is obesity. In large measure, the cause is inadequate supervision of children's eating habits. If children, and subsequently teenagers, choose high-carbohydrate foods—snack foods, sweets, etc.—they are hungry more often and consequently eat several times a day. Many teenagers don't drink enough milk and don't eat enough fruits and vegetables. They probably don't get enough ascorbic acid, and they may not get an adequate proportion of amino acids.

Faulty diet is particularly serious for girls, who carry the responsibility for bearing children. A malnourished mother is ill-equipped to deliver a healthy baby, particularly if she also smokes and drinks alcohol. For this reason it is especially important for young women to receive counseling in nutrition. It is a healthy trend that more schools and universities are now offering nutritional instructions. In addition, many schools are making an effort to substitute wholesome, satisfying foods for the potato chips and candies that provide nothing but empty calories. More effort is needed in this direction.

3.

Food Additives and Illness

In the western world there has been a great interest during recent years in the whole question of food additives and their possible effects on people's health. Frightening stories appear with great regularity in the news media, giving rise to much concern and misunderstanding amongst a public that is not particularly well educated in science and scientific method.

One of the key "panic" words is, of course, cancer. The number of people dying of cancer *is* on the increase. But it's important to remember that recent total increases have been due mainly to lung cancer. If we exclude lung cancer deaths from the death rates, we find that the overall cancer death rates remain fairly constant. This means that in spite of the exposures to vast numbers of chemicals we are not now dying more commonly of cancer than we did 25 or 50 years ago. The cancer from which we are dying in relatively large numbers is lung cancer, produced mainly by cigaret smoking.

There is no doubt that cancer is a serious disease, and we do know that certain elements in our environment do influence and act to initiate cancer. Some of these elements are man-made, while others exist in nature. We should remember that there are natural carcinogens in foodstuffs; sunlight can cause skin cancer, particularly in blonds and redheads; and in some parts of the world there is a great deal of natural radiation that can cause cancer.

Because cancer is a serious and frightening disease, it is also an emotional issue. People take up positions, and they battle valiantly for various causes, and especially against various chemicals. As Dr. H. B. Morley has recently pointed out, lawyers now speak as scientists, sociologists pontificate as toxicologists, biochemists declaim as politicians, and everyone is now an expert in someone else's field. In North America, particularly, many people presumably have nothing else to do but to worry about limited or non-existent problems—especially in regard to the question of possible toxicants in foods. Obviously it's a good idea to police additives in our food, but the possible dangers inherent in additives presently being used are usually greatly overstated.

We should be watchful and wary but not crudely intolerant in these matters.

The Dose of Chemicals

One of the most important points to recognize about any chemical, drug, or carcinogen is that the dose is extremely important. If the dose of a chemical is extremely small—say, one part per million—the chances are that it will have no effect whatsoever. If the dose is large, its effect will become more obvious. This is especially true in drugs used for therapeutic purposes. For example, in certain types of heart disease, 0.25 mg of Digoxin per day is a therapeutic dose. If we use 20 times this dose, the patient will die. Obviously, then, Digoxin is a poison—in a large dose. Used in a therapeutic dose, it is a very important and useful drug.

Food Poisoning

An additional fear about food additives is that they may cause food poisoning. A look at the facts may allay some of this apprehension. In the United States the Food and Drug Administration has listed and ranked the sources of food hazards or food poisonings. What most people do not know, and what the news media have not often discussed, is that microbiological contamination is the first and greatest cause of food poisoning. In the United States it has been estimated that food-borne disease attacks 10 million people every year. The leading causes are *Salmonellae* and *Staphylococci*. They can grow in foods and they produce severe symptoms of food poisoning, often passed off as "intestinal flu." It's important to remember this: The biggest hazard from food is from microbiological causes, mainly bacteria. This fascinating subject is discussed at length in a later chapter.

The second-largest food hazard is poor nutrition, ranging from overeating or gluttony, with resulting obesity, to a poor choice of foods, with resultant nutrient deficiencies, to simply not enough food. There is a contradiction here: Far too much food, which is a common situation in North America and the western world, coexisting with situations of too little food or too few of the essential vitamins. We know that overeating does have harmful effects, particularly in regard to cardiovascular disease and diabetes.

The third-largest hazard in food is accidental environmental contamination. For example, polybrominated biphenyls (PBPs) entered the food supply chain some years ago when they were used by mistake in cattle feed in Michigan. In Iran and Iraq mercury-treated grain intended for use as seed was mistakenly used as food, with devastating effects; there have been other cases of mercury exposure in lakes and streams in parts of Canada and the United States. Illnesses from situations and accidents like these are rare, anywhere in the world.

Fourth on the list of food hazards are the toxicants that occur naturally in foods. One of these is amygdalin or laetrile, which is present in apricot seeds; these seeds also contain an enzyme that liberates hydrocyanic acid. There have been cases of cyanide poisoning in people who ate apricot seed milkshakes prepared according to a guru in the health-food literature. Amygdalin and certain other natural toxic chemical substances appear in many crop plants, including almonds and lima beans. Growers and plant breeders have selected strains of these which are low in these compounds.

Aflatoxins are carcinogenic substances produced by common molds or fungi that grow on farm crops such as corn, soybeans, and peanuts. The FDA has set a tolerance limit of 20 parts per billion for aflatoxin in food for human consumption. At this level it can produce cancer in certain laboratory animals. It may well be that the high prevalence of primary carcinoma of the liver found in certain parts of Africa is due in part to aflatoxin poisoning, because in Africa and Asia where foods are not stored properly, many of them, if not all, are contaminated by these poisonous fungi. We will discuss these and other natural poisons in food in a later chapter.

Last on the FDA's list of food hazards are the hazards from pesticide residues in foods and from food additives. Harm from these chemicals is rare. We know that many billions of pounds of pesticides have been used in food crops, and so far there is no evidence that there has been human injury or death from a pesticide residue in food. (We are speaking here of the normal residue on food, not of accidental contamination by large amounts of pesticide.) Modern food additives are regularly tested, not only by government departments in Canada and the United States, but also by chemical companies that make new pesticides and new food additivies.

The point is that, despite all the recent excitement in the news media, there is no evidence that anybody has been killed by residues of pesticides in foodstuffs or by food additives themselves.

During the last 20 years laws and regulations for new food additives have included extensive toxicity tests. Obviously it is almost impossible to test all the possible effects of every single chemical—there are limits to money, to laboratories, and to the number of people devoted to this objective. But we can take comfort from knowing that so far the human race has eaten those foods that are not poisonous. Every now and again, of course, mistakes are made. Food sometimes do contain toxic substances, but we generally keep our intakes below the toxic level.

Apart from chemical additives in foods, there are other substances that have caused a great deal of talk during recent years—diethylstilbestrol, for example. This hormone has been implanted under the skin of beef animals in order to make them grow more rapidly. There has been a finding that some cases of vaginal carcinoma appeared in young women whose mothers had taken diethylstilbestrol while pregnant. One group of women received 12.3 g of diethylstilbestrol while pregnant. Although no cases of cancer have been found in their daughters, some vaginal adenosis was observed, and it is known that this can be a pre-cancerous lesion. These cases are relatively rare, but even so it is understandable that there is concern about intake of the hormone in our food. Let's look at the facts.

We know that if diethylstilbestrol is implanted under the skin of cattle, sometimes it can be found in traces in the livers of the animals but not in the muscle meat. In experiments it has been determined that when cattle are *fed* large doses of diethylstilbestrol, there is always about 10 times as much of this substance found in the liver than in the muscle of the animal. When cattle have been given the hormone by approved methods—that is, implanted under the skin—it is not detectable at all in the muscle meat. In a survey carried out by the U.S. Department of Agriculture from 1973 to 1975, none of this substance was detectable in muscle meat, and there were less than five parts per billion in 8241 of 8293 liver samples examined, a negligible amount in beef cattle.

In another experiment the hormone was made radioactive and pellets of radioactive diethylstilbestrol implanted in the cattle's ears. A level of radioactivity corresponding to 0.12 parts per million of diethylstilbestrol was found in the livers of these cattle. The level detected in this trial is such that 100,000 tons of beef liver would contain 12.3 g of diethylstilbestrol, the dose received by each pregnant woman in the study mentioned earlier.

Artificial sweeteners are another area of concern and controversy. The information about both cyclamates and saccharin is by no means clear. The current opinion seems to be that cyclamates do not produce tumors in people and that the dose for saccharin to produce tumors in human beings would have to be very high indeed. In fact, studies of diabetics who have used saccharin extensively have not shown saccharin to produce cancer in humans. Those who wish an outright ban on cyclamates and saccharin should produce evidence that these substances in the doses used have produced cancer in humans. Such evidence is not forthcoming. The Select Committee on sugar substitutes of the American Diabetes Association started a review of scientific data in July 1977. They found that in 12 epidemiologic studies of artificial sweetener consumption and bladder cancer risks, only one reported that saccharin usage had significantly increased the risk for bladder cancer, and this investigation was criticized for defects in methods of analysis. The 11 remaining studies showed no association between saccharin and malignancy.

The U.S. Food and Drug Administration has concluded that such epidemiologic studies cannot detect weak carcinogens; however, the FDA feels that there is neither evidence to accept nor reject the hypothesis that the use of artificial sweetners, specifically saccharin, increases the risk of bladder cancer in humans. The American Diabetes Association has concluded that much more research, with a broader scope and greater detail, is needed before the saccharin controversy can be resolved. They feel that, based on the existing evidence, there appears to be little justification for placing governmental restrictions on the use of saccharin. People who are worried about saccharin should not use it. This substance has been used for a long time by a lot of people. Had it been obviously carcinogenic, we would have known it by now.

The question of nitrates in processed meats is of considerable public interest. We know that nitrates in bacon, for example, can be converted to nitrosamines during frying. We also know that nitrosamines may be carcinogenic to various species of laboratory animals at low rates of dosage. But nitrosamines can be formed in the stomach by a reaction between secondary amines and nitrites, and most of the nitrites in the stomach originate in the saliva. Furthermore, many common vegetables, particularly lettuce, beets, celery, and spinach, are high in nitrates, which are reduced to nitrites by intestinal bacteria. In one investigation high levels were found in "organic carrots" grown on muck soil. Therefore, to try to eliminate the use of nitrates and nitrites in meats does not seem to be a very useful objective, because these same chemicals are found in many other foods. In addition, nitrites and nitrates perform a very useful function in inhibiting the growth of botulism organisms in cured meats. We should probably not become too complacent about the existence of nitrosamines and nitrites, but we shouldn't let hysteria in the news media stampede us in the wrong direction.

The whole question of nitrosamines and nitrites is under active investigation, and within the next few years we will know much more about it. We do know that vitamin E and vitamin C are antioxidants and that antioxidants inhibit the formation of nitrosamines. Possibly a simple solution for those people who are worried about nitrosamines is to eat more vitamin C and vitamin E. Certainly there is no point in banning nitrites and nitrates at the present time.

Food Additives

Under legislation in both Canada and the United States, food additives are carefully defined: "Any substance, the intended use of which results or may reasonably be expected to result directly or indirectly in its becoming a component or otherwise affecting the characteristics of any food."

This definition of a food additive is restricted to substances generally recognized to be safe under the conditions of its intended use. There is a list, which is frequently modified, called the GRAS list (Generally Recognized as Safe). Substances on the list are under continual review, but for general working purposes they are regarded as safe. It should also be pointed out that the term "food additive" does not include pesticides, color additives, animal drugs such as diethylstilbestrol. There are certain other legal exceptions.

Public Opinion

Recently in Canada the Department of Health and Welfare surveyed opinions about food additives, with interesting results.

Many of the respondents felt that the information contained on the labels of foodstuffs was not satisfactory. This is obviously true; most people are untrained in chemistry, and the lists of chemicals on food packages are therefore bewildering. They felt that colors were incompletely listed on the labels (there is currently an obsession with food coloring in North America). Many people thought that pesticides were food additives. They are not, but obviously pesticides are present in very small amounts, so people wondered whether they should be listed on labels. The public considered the term ''additive'' in a broader sense than the Canadian government definitions. Only a small percentage of the respondents recognized the potential benefits of additives. Many perceived them as inevitably harmful, and many felt that the use of food additives and food coloring was unjustifiable. They expressed the opinion that health could be negatively affected by colors in food. Many consumers indicated a willingness to pay more money for food that was free of additives, even though food without additives would decay much more rapidly. Furthermore, experience has shown that additives do not cause health problems amongst the general population. But these facts are disregarded, for the question of additives has become an emotional one.

People perceive that additives are bad, largely because the news media have succeeded in frightening the public. Media attention is good insofar as it alerts people to an area of concern. But in this case, interest has been diverted away from the main cause of food poisoning, bacterial contamination. The net result of all this information from the news media has been to give an inaccurate and rather biased view of the risks from foods. On the other hand, in a society that is heavily involved in the production of vast numbers of new chemicals, it is right that the public should be worried about what they eat and what is shed into their water supplies.

The Question of Risks

When we consider toxicological risks in our food, we should put the matter in perspective. How do these risks compare with others in our lives? Dr. Bernard Oser, a man of vast experience in chemistry, and particularly in food additives, has recently produced a paper on this subject of risks. He has classified them (Table 3:1) in terms of whether they are voluntary or involuntary. The riskiest occupation in our society is motorcy-

TABLE 3:1

RISK CLASSIFICATION AS TO VOLUNTARY AND INVOLUNTARY*

Activity	Risk of death per million persons per year
Voluntary	
Smoking 20 cigarets per day	5,000
Drinking one bottle of wine per day	75
Playing football	40
Car racing	1,200
Rock climbing	140
Car driving	170
Motorcycling	20,000
Taking contraceptive pills	20
Involuntary	
Run over by road vehicle (U.S.)	50
Run over by road vehicle (U.K.)	60
Floods (U.S.)	2.2
Earthquake (California)	1.7
Tornadoes (Midwest U.S.)	2.2
Storms (U.S.)	0.8
Lightning (U.K.)	0.1
Falling aircraft (U.S.)	0.1
Falling aircraft (U.K.)	0.02
Explosion of pressure vessel (U.S.)	0.05
Release from atomic power station at site boundary (U.S.)	0.1
Release from atomic power station at 1km (U.K.)	0.1
Flooding of dikes (Holland)	0.1
Bites of venomous creatures (U.K.)	0.2

TABLE 3:1 (continued)

RISK CLASSIFICATION AS TO VOLUNTARY AND INVOLUNTARY*

Activity	Risk of death per million persons per year
Transport of petrol and chemicals (U.S.)	0.05
Transport of petrol and chemicals (U.K.)	0.02
Leukemia	80
Influenza	200
Meteorite	0.00006
Cosmic rays from explosion of supernovae	0.01-0.00001

*Adapted from Kletz (1977)

Source: Oser, B. L. (1978) Benefit/Risk: Whose? What? How Much? Food Technology. Reprint August pp. 55–58.

cling. This is followed by smoking 20 cigarets a day and by car racing. Very low on the list are releases from atomic power stations and the flooding of dikes in Holland. Even lower are the risks of possibilities of damage from cosmic rays. It would appear that at the moment the public is very interested in situations that are not particularly risky. The following Table 3:2 shows the usual risks of various types of activity. The

TABLE 3:2

RISK OF DEATH CLASSIFIED BY TYPE OF ACTIVITY*

Activity	Risk of death per million persons per year
Travel	
Pedestrian	40
Motorcycling	20,000
Automobile	20–30
Airplane	9

TABLE 3:2 (continued)

RISK OF DEATH CLASSIFIED BY THE TYPE OF ACTIVITY*

Activity	Risk of death per million persons per year
Sports	
Canoeing	400
Power boating	30
Drowning	19–30
Skiing	170
Rock climbing	1,000
Bicycling	10
Car racing	1,200
Eating or Drinking	
Alcohol[b]—one bottle of wine per day	75
Alcohol[b]—one bottle of beer per day	20
Aflatoxin[b]—4 tbsp of peanut butter per day	40
Aflatoxin[b]—1 pt of milk per day	10
Charcoal broiled steak[b]—½ lb per week	0.4
Miscellaneous	
Smoking 20 cigarets per day	2,000–5,000
Falls	70–90
Home accidents	12
Contraceptive pills	20
Abortion after 14 weeks	70
Pregnancy	230
Vaccination against smallpox	3
Hurricanes	0.4
Lightning	0.1–0.05
Earthquakes (California)	1.7

*Based on statistical data from various sources, chiefly in the U.S. and U.K.
[b]Risk of cancer only
Source: Oser, B. L. (1979) Benefit/Risk: Whose? What? How Much? Food Technology. Reprint August pp. 55–58.

TABLE 3:3

CLASSIFICATION OF GRAS SUBSTANCES BY TECHNICAL EFFECT*

Anticaking agents, free-flow agents

Antioxidants

Colors, coloring adjuncts (including color stabilizers, color fixatives, color-retention agents, etc.)

Curing, pickling agents

Dough conditioners (including yeast foods)

Drying agents

Emulsifiers (see surface-active agents), emulsifier salts

Enzymes

Firming agents

Flavor enhancers

Flavoring agents, adjuvants

Flour-testing agents (including bleaching and maturing agents)

Formulation aids (including carriers, binders, fillers, plasticizers, film-formers, tabletting aids, etc.)

Fumigants

Humectants, moisture-retention agents, anti-dusting agents

Leavening agents

Lubricants, release agents

Non-nutritive sweeteners

Nutrient supplements

pH control agents (including buffers, acids, alkalies, neutralizing agents)

Preservatives (including antimicrobial agents, fungistats, mold and rope inhibitors, etc.)

Processing aids (including clarifying agents, clouding agents, catalysts, flocculants, filter aids, etc.)

Propellants, aerating agents, gases

Sequestrants

Solvents, vehicles

Stabilizers, thickeners (including suspending and bodying agents, setting agents, gelling agents, bulking agents, etc.)

Surface-active agents other than emulsifiers (including solubilizing agents, dispersants, detergents, wetting agents, rehydration enhancers, whipping agents, foaming agents, defoaming agents, etc.)

Surface-finishing agents (including glazes, polishes, waxes, protective coatings)

TABLE 3:3 (continued)

CLASSIFICATION OF GRAS SUBSTANCES BY TECHNICAL EFFECT*

Synergists
Texturizers

---

*Prepared by the Food Protection Committee of the National Academy of Sciences/ National Research Council and later adopted by the Food and Drug Administration with the addition of non-nutritive sweeteners and nutritive sweeteners (source: Code of Federal Regulations Section 170.3)
Source: Oser, B. L. (1978) Benefit/Risk: Whose? What? How Much? Food Technology. Reprint August pp. 55–58.

dangers of alcohol, for example, are considerably greater than the dangers of aflatoxins, and pregnancy is a considerably greater risk than alcoholism. Notice that risks from food additives are so low as not to appear at all in Table 3:2. The risk of death from charcoal-broiled steak at the rate of ½ (0.25 kg) pound per week is 0.4 million persons per year, something similar to the risk of deaths from hurricanes.

It is reasonable to conclude, from the information we currently have available, that the risks of death from food additives are somewhat less than negligible.

The Uses of Food Additives

Table 3:3 lists the food additives known as GRAS (Generally Regarded as Safe) substances and the purposes they serve— what food additives are supposed to do. Table 3:4 illustrates some of the benefits of food additives, which we will discuss in more detail later in this chapter. It's important to realize that food additives are used for specific purposes. However, the public has the right to ask whether all the food additives are necessary, and manufacturers should be able to answer this question. They should not use chemicals in foods that are not necessary.

The British government has a very sensible approach to food additives. Their Food Additives and Contaminants Committee (FACC) must be satisfied that there is a real technical advantage to be gained for the consumer by the use of a

TABLE 3:4

BENEFITS OF FOOD ADDITIVES AND WHO RECEIVES THEM

Benefit	Recipient		
	Producer	Consumer	Society
Processing aid (pH control, emulsifying, maturing, leavening, anti-caking, and curing agents, enzymes, humectants, lubricants, etc.)	x	x	
Nutrition (vitamins, minerals, amino acids)		x	x
Preservation (preservatives, antioxidants, fumigants, etc., preserve against spoilage or deterioration caused by bacteria, mold, oxidation, autolysis, etc.)	x	x	x
Stabilization (thickening, clarifying, firming, and chelating agents)	x	x	
Variety (seasonal and geographic availability)		x	x
Hedonics (flavor, taste, texture, color, bleaching, anti-clouding, and foaming agents)		x	
Sanitation (canning, packaging, wrapping)	x	x	x
Convenience (prepared mixes, doughs, pre-baking, pre-cooking, propellants)		x	x
Economy		x	x

Source: Oser, B. L. (1978) Benefit/Risk: Whose? What? How Much? Food Technology. Reprint August pp. 55–58.

particular additive: That the food will have an improved shelf life; that it will be less hazardous from a microbiological point of view; that the addition will materially reduce the cost of production; or that the food can be made more attractive and appealing.

Food Coloring

At the present time in North America food coloring is the center of a storm of controversy because of claims made by Dr. Ben Feingold that it is implicated in some cases of hyper-activity in children. Why use artificial colors at all? Because we expect foods to have certain colors. We expect a strawberry-flavored drink to have what we think of as a strawberry color. Furthermore, color also helps to standardize the appearance of a product; it makes foods look better, appeals to the sales value, and no doubt may stimulate the appetite. There is no absolute need for food coloring; presumably there is no absolute need for music, either. But in our society people expect certain colors, and they have become accustomed to them. In fact, they don't buy foods that aren't the expected color. In nature, tomatoes, for example, don't always have the same color; they vary according to the variety of tomato and the climatic and soil conditions in which the plants are grown. But we have come to the conclusion that ketchup has to be a certain color, and that is the ketchup we will buy.

Food color can be classified in three groups: Natural colors of either vegetables or fruits; synthetic organic compounds; and mineral or synthetic inorganic colors. Among the natural food colors is dried algae meal, fed to chickens in order to promote a yellow skin on the chicken and yellow egg yolks. Annatto, which is from the seed pods of a plant called *Bixa orellana,* was the first food color approved by the United States Congress for the coloring of butter, in 1886. It is quite obvious that if butter were to be marketed in an uncolored form it would be considerably less attractive, just as margarine sold in its original white color lacked much appeal.

Other natural colors are yellow from the Aztec marigold, red from dried beet powder, and caramel from heated sugars. An interesting one is carmine, which is derived from an insect called *Coccus cacti.* Only female insects are used, and one pound of carmine requires approximately 70,000 of them. (Carmine must be pasteurized before use to clear it of salmonella organisms.) Carotene and cottonseed flour give a yellow color, chlorophyl green. Grape skin extract produces a purple color; paprika is, of course, red; and the yellow of saffron is a very expensive color from the stigma of the *Crocus sativus*. Other natural colors come from titanium oxide, a mineral; aquamarine blue, from the mineral lapis lazuli; and various vegetable juices. In many situations, synthetic colors are more stable and function more efficiently than natural ones. For instance, beet powder, which is used to color tomato paste, is not efficient, because its color is not fast and it cakes during storage. One of the big disadvantages of natural colors is that they break down under changes in air, heat, and light.

Synthetic food colors are primarily coal tar dyes. Since 1912, 625 of them have been synthesized. At present in the United States 10 of these dyes are used as coloring agents for food. They are FD and C Blue No. 1, FD and C Blue No. 2, FD and C Green No. 3, FD and C Red No. 3, FD and C Red No. 4, FD and C Yellow No. 5, FD and C Yellow No. 6, Citrus Red No. 2, and Orange B. The well-known FD and C Red No. 2 or amaranth was banned in the United States in 1976, although it is still legal in Canada. Red Dye No. 4 is used only in maraschino cherries, at levels not exceeding 150 parts per million; Citrus No. 2 is used to dye the skins of oranges at two parts per million; Orange B is used in sausage casings at 150 parts per million.

The saga of amaranth, Red Dye 2, reads like a Victorian melodrama. Finally, as far as we can gather, its withdrawal in the United States was for political, rather than scientific, reasons. Passionate sides have been taken on this issue, and scientific objectivity seems to have gone by the board. Numerous experiments have been undertaken, but criticisms of the findings have included lack of good statistical design, lack of the appropriate breed of rats, and lack of sufficient numbers. Further, in all the experiments that have been undertaken, there remains the question of whether all the rats were placed on the same basic diet. To complicate matters still further, in any research of this nature, the interpretation of results is always open to question. There is variability in the opinions of pathologists as to whether the tissue they are studying is cancerous or not. Probably the last word on Red Dye 2 has not been spoken.

What we await are more well-designed clinical trials that are not fueled by emotion and political considerations.

If mothers do not wish to expose their children to food dyes, they should take note of the following list. The substances that contain most food dyes are, in order of magnitude:

1. beverages
2. candy, confections
3. dessert powders
4. bakery goods
5. sausage (casing color)
6. cereals
7. dairy foods—ice cream, sherbet, butter, cheese
8. snack foods
9. maraschino cherries

In this list the only foods that children actually need are butter and cheese. Mothers can make most of the other items without using food coloring. Children certainly do not need highly colored beverages, candy and confections, and dessert powders. If mothers make their own cakes from primary products, there need be no dyes in the bakery goods. For that matter, it's possible to make sausage at home without colored casings, and children can eat home-cooked oatmeal instead of dry cereals. They do not need snack foods, and certainly their intake of maraschino cherries can be eliminated.

Flavors in Foods

The world of flavorings is an enchanted land, because flavor plays a very important part in our appreciation of food and in stimulating the appetite. Associated with flavor is, of course, aroma. People who do not have a sense of smell do not taste their foods as well as those who have. We know that there are four basic flavors: sweet, salt, sour, and bitter. Subtle combinations of these four elements result in an enormous variety of flavors.

The idea of "natural" flavors has great appeal. But what's natural? A flavor that occurs in nature? Natural flavors include many herbs and spices—allspice, basil, bay leaves, ginger, horseradish, pepper, turmeric, tarragon, thyme, and many more. Don't fall into the trap of assuming that all these natural spices are harmless. Large doses of nutmeg, for example, are hallucinogenic, and very high doses can cause liver damage and death. Nutmeg is not usually abused, because even in fairly small amounts it can cause severe headache, cramps, and nausea. But it's well to remember that even in "natural" foods the wrong dosage can be harmful.

In many instances natural flavors can be copied exactly by a substance made in the laboratory. The sour taste of citric acid found in a lemon is exactly the same as the sour taste of citric acid made in the laboratory. There is no difference between the two. On the other hand, natural flavors may be very complex. A typical apple flavor, for instance, comprises at least 88 chemicals—among them acetaldehyde, citric acid, acetone, benzoic acid, diacetyl ethanol, ethyl butyrate, furfural, hexanol, propanal, and propyl acetate. Obviously, if we push things to the extreme and attach a label like that to every apple, most people would feel ill just contemplating it.

Regulations in the United States, Canada, and other countries stipulate that labels on food must show whether added flavors are natural or synthetic; if they are synthetic, their chemical nature must be stated. Unfortunately, people often do not understand what the chemical names mean, and in fact many people retire in confusion and fright when they see a chemical name. This tendency to panic can only be controlled by more knowledge.

There are vast numbers of different flavors and different arrangements of existing flavors, and every year many more new chemicals are discovered for use as flavoring in foods. In general any new substance has to be subjected to toxicological tests. As we have stated, however, toxicology is not an exact science. Furthermore, since flavorings are used in very small amounts, it is in general rather improbable that they would be harmful. Chemicals or drugs in very small amounts usually do not influence the metabolism of the living cell. There are exceptions, of course, but the general principle is that if a dose is extremely small—that is, in parts per billion—it is improbable that there will be an effect.

Flavor Enhancers

Associated with flavors are substances that enhance flavor. The commonest one is table salt, but monosodium glutamate is more powerful. The Japanese discovered it in dried seaweed and have been using it for hundreds of years. In the United States about 150 million pounds per year are consumed. The glutamic acid component of monosodium glutamate is a common amino acid found in many foodstuffs. And the glutamic acid in the foods is changed into monosodium glutamate in the human body. Those who complain about the addition of monosodium glutamate to foods should understand that this substance is also formed within the human body; at a reasonable dosage it should not be considered dangerous.

It is reasonably well known that monosodium glutamate can in certain people produce the Chinese Restaurant Syndrome, with symptoms including chest pains, headaches, a burning sensation, and facial pressure. This is an allergic response peculiar to certain people, not a general condition affecting everyone. Obviously, if one is sensitive to MSG, one should avoid it.

Synthetic Foods

In the future there is no doubt that, as natural products become prohibitively expensive or even completely unobtainable, more imitation meat and imitation dairy products will be developed. This whole question of synthetic foods is a matter of some concern to those of us who cling to the foods we are used to, produced in the traditional way. It is difficult to define what a natural food is, but many people hope that we will be able to continue to eat them. However, rapid population growth and a continual decrease in agricultural land are necessitating the synthesis of all kinds of new foods.

Natural Foods

How do we define "natural foods?" If we apply artificial fertilizers to the wheat crop, pesticides to kill the insects that eat the wheat crop, and fungicides to kill the fungi that may destroy or contaminate the wheat crop, have we then produced a "natural" food? If we used cow manure or horse manure as a fertilizer, could we then claim to have produced a "natural food"? In fact, it could be argued that there is no such thing. All the foods we eat have been considerably modified by genetic manipulation, by the breeding of different varieties, and by the application of scientific method in their production. Our foods are the results of scientific and technological development— natural, yet modified by humans. Perhaps the only "natural" foods are the wild berries, wild grains, and wild animals that our ancestors ate.

Food Additive Safety

Toxicology is not an exact science, and animal experiments do not necessarily indicate what will happen when humans consume specific chemicals. It's important to remember, though, that food additives are used in very small amounts, so that the likelihood of their causing harm is correspondingly small. Obviously, any substance intended for widespread consumption must be subject to careful scrutiny, but we must maintain a sense of proportion. Neither governments nor food manufacturers would deliberately allow poisonous materials to be put into food.

According to Dr. Philipp E. Shubick from the Epply Institute for Research in Cancer, University of Nebraska Medical Center, the substances allowed for use as food additives, as far as toxicologists can tell and as far as carcinogenic risk is concerned, have been well investigated. There are, of course, limits to the amount of money and effort that we can spend on the investigation of chemicals. There are other, more important things to do in a modern state, particularly as it has not been shown that people have been harmed by food additives. Such evidence may arise, but so far there is no such evidence.

Even among banned substances, the evidence of potential harm is sketchy. Red Dye No. 2, mentioned previously, is a case in point. It has not been demonstrated to be toxic. It has been banned in the United States because it has not been demonstrated to be safe to the satisfaction of the Commissioner of Food and Drugs. Cyclamate is another example, It has not been demonstrated to be carcinogenic. It does produce a metabolite, cyclohexylamine, which can cause testicular atrophy in rats. We cannot be absolutely certain, but we assume that in very small doses cyclamate will not be harmful in humans. The story about saccharin is not clear, either. When it is given at a level of 15 per cent—a very high level—to male rats for two generations, it causes bladder cancer. But we still don't understand why this is so, and, as mentioned earlier, epidemiological studies have shown that saccharin does not pose a major cancer risk in humans. For people who worry about either saccharin or cyclamate, the solution is very simple: Don't use them.

One category of additives comprises those that are a result of processing, as opposed to those that are intentionally added to foods. For instance, the technique of smoking foods has been known for many thousands of years. Smoked foods have been associated with a higher incidence of gastric cancer in the Baltic states and in Iceland, although there are no adequate data to support this contention. We do know that smoked foods contain carcinogens. Artificial smoke flavoring, on the other hand, contains no carcinogens. This should give "natural food" advocates pause for thought: The natural process contains carcinogens, while the chemical process that provides a smoke flavor does not. In fact, the relationship between cooking processes and the production of carcinogens has received far too little attention and demands further study.

The Importance of Additives

Additives are placed in foods for a number of specific reasons:
1. to improve or maintain nutritional value

2. to enhance quality
3. to reduce waste
4. to enhance consumer acceptance
5. to improve keeping quality
6. to make food more readily available
7. to facilitate food preparation.

The public wants foods of good texture and good flavor, foods that remain in that condition for as long as possible. They want cakes to be moist, they want pickles to maintain their color and be crisp. These things can only be accomplished by careful use of selected food additives.

If we had no additives in our foods many unpleasant things would happen. Foods would rot much more rapidly than they do now. Flour and cake mixes would be quickly infested with grubs and insects. Many foods would look unappetizing because they would have no color; pickles would be soft and yellow; baked goods would all look alike because they would have no color. Some new products could not be made at all; if the additive called sugar weren't used, we couldn't make jam or marmalade. Without doubt, food additives prevent many severe problems in food production and preservation.

We need leavening agents so that commercial bakers can have an eight-hour day, because leavening agents work quickly. We need flavors and enhancers to add to foods' sensory appeal; starches and emulsifiers are thickening agents that are essential to gravy, sauces, and dressings. And some people like carbon dioxide to put fizz in their pop or in their Scotch. So before we become too excited about food additives we must consider their uses and we must consider in what amounts they are eaten.

A recent study looked at the amounts of 1830 additives consumed on average per year. The median intake per person per year is 0.5 mg; in other words, 915 of the additives are eaten at levels above 0.5 mg annually, and 915 are consumed in amounts smaller than 0.5 mg. To put these quantities in proportion, 0.5 mg is about the weight of a grain of salt. Of all the additives used, sugar is the most commonly consumed, at a rate of about 100 pounds or about 45 kg per person per annum. Salt is next at 15 pounds (6.8 kg), then corn syrup and dextrose at 8.4 pounds (3.9 kg) and 4.2 pounds (1.8 kg) respectively. Another 32 additives are consumed in amounts of about 9 pounds or 4 kg per person yearly. The remainder, about 1800 in number, are eaten at the yearly rate of less than one pound or 0.5 kg per person, most of them considerably less.

It is quite obvious that additives should only be added to foods if they are needed. But if they are used correctly, they are a great blessing to our already very comfortable society. We should be aware, however, of some of the inappropriate uses of food additives:

1. to disguise faulty or inferior processes
2. to conceal damaged, spoiled, or inferior goods
3. to deceive consumers
4. to gain some functional property at the expense of nutritional quality
5. to substitute for economical, well recognized, good manufacturing processes and practices
6. to use in amounts in excess of the minimum requirement to achieve the intended effects.

Preservatives

Food preservation has been practiced for thousands of years, ever since it was discovered that the fall harvest of grain could be used to sustain people throughout the winter. Grain storage pits were used in the ancient valley civilizations of the Indus, Tigris, Euphrates, and the Nile. In other parts of the world food was, and still is, stored in woven baskets. The problem of insect damage was a major one; in many parts of Africa and Asia today, one-third to one-half of the grain is destroyed by insects and rodents. It is only in the last 50 years or so that effective methods have been developed to preserve grain in elevators.

As far as we know, the early Romans were the first to use ice and snow to preserve perishable foods. The ancient Egyptians practiced salting and sun drying to protect their foods. Other peoples preserved foods by submerging them in oil. In the Middle East and in Central Europe sliced apples were strung and dried, and grapes, figs, dates, almonds, apricots, and walnuts were dried and kept for winter use. Pear and apple juices were fermented. The monasteries refined methods of preserving meat, fish, fruits, and vegetables. The standard methods in ancient days were smoking, drying, and salting. Milk was preserved by being made into cheese. Mustard, now used as a condiment, was used in early times as a preservative; the Romans used large quantities of it to preserve fruit juices.

Natural Preservatives

Some foods possess naturally occurring preservatives. Green bananas contain an antifungal compound, cabbage an antibiotic, and some cereals a fungicide. Egg white contains a substance called conalbumin that inhibits the anthrax bacillus as well as having antifungal properties. Garlic contains an antibiotic, while honey, which has long been used to heal wounds, contains a substance that helps to produce hydrogen peroxide, which kills bacteria. There may also be other antibiotics in honey. Milk contains an antibiotic, as do onions, radishes, tomatoes, strawberries, and sweet potatoes. Many spices and essential oils, containing both antibiotic and antifungal agents, have been used as preservatives. It is interesting that these antibiotics exist in nature; what we have done in making drugs like penicillin, streptomycin, and many others is to take the antibiotics out of their natural production, concentrate them, and use them therapeutically. Most of our antibiotics are derived from fungi.

Some of the traditional methods of preserving foods have involved fermentation. During this process, certain microorganisms—bacteria—produce acids and other chemical substances that stop putrefaction or deterioration in foods. In cheese production the milk has been fermented, as it has in the manufacture of acidolphilus milk or yogurt. Other examples of preservation by fermentation include the making of sauerkraut, pickles, and green olives. These fermentation processes, although they occur naturally, must be meticulously controlled by skilled people, whose art reaches perhaps its finest point with the production of fine wines and other alcoholic drinks.

Antioxidants

Antioxidants are another kind of preservative, some occurring naturally in foods. The commonest of these are ascorbic acid or vitamin C and tocopherols of the vitamin E complex. There are also many other antioxidants. Onions, for instance, contain one, and red wines contain anthocyanin pigments, which are antioxidants. However, these days synthetic antioxidants are often used, as they can withstand the temperatures used in food processing. The substances most commonly used are propyl gallate and butylated hydroxyanisole (BHA) and butylated hydroxytoluene (BHT), particularly in dry breakfast cereals, instant potato flakes, dehydrated potato shreds, and so on. Some people have become rather suspicious of BHT, although after a great deal of research work it would appear that this material is not harmful to human health. As far as we know, BHA and propyl gallate are not harmful either, although the future may tell whether these substances have risks attached to them. Interestingly enough, it might well be that antioxidants have some role in preventing or stalling old age.

Emulsifiers and Stabilizers

These chemicals bind the substances from which food is made and thicken it. Without them, cakes would fall apart, process cheese would melt, and puddings would be thin syrups. There could be no milk substitutes and there could be no custard or banana cream pie. Shortening fats would be thin and oily, mayonnaise would separate into its various original constituents—the oil and water would not mix to form an emulsion. There would be no ice cream, as it would consist of a mass of ice crystals. The emulsifiers have one primary function, and that is to bind water and oil or fat together and keep them together. Milk and soybeans contain one of the common natural emulsifiers, lecithin; another natural emulsifier is cholesterol.

In addition to the natural emulsifiers, a large number of synthetic chemicals are available to do this job. The common one is polysorbate 60. Others include acetylated monoglycerides, calcium caprylate, cholic acid, and other similar materials derived from ox bile. Also in this group is disodium phosphate. It is not necessary to go into a great deal of chemical detail on emulsifiers, except to say how necessary they are in the preparation of modern foods.

Stabilizers bind the ingredients together and smooth the texture of foods. They put body into puddings and sauces and gravies, they stabilize the foam in beer, and they add bulk to special dietary foods. Some stabilizers are natural, others synthetic. Among the natural ones are the gums of certain trees—gum arabic, gum tragacanth, and arabinogalactin. Some other common stabilizers are agar agar, calcium alginate, locust bean gum, methyl-cellulose, and propylene glycol alginate. Many of the stabilizers are made from seaweed, one of the best known being carrageenan. This substance has been used for hundreds of years in Ireland, where the people of Carragheen first used it in their puddings. However, we are not altogether certain about its safety as a food additive. In fairly large doses in rats it has produced liver lesions, but here again the question of dosage is of great importance. It is highly improbable that any humans would eat carrageenan at a level of 2.5 to 5.0 per cent of their diet. The general opinion is that in the doses usually used, this material is not harmful. If it were, we are sure that the people of Carragheen over a period of a few hundred years would have noticed that something was wrong.

Accidental Contaminants: Toxic Metals

Apart from the various substances that are deliberately added to foods, there are materials that may get into foods accidentally. As far back as 1767 Sir George Baker, M.D., wrote an excellent account of the endemic colic of Devonshire. Upon studying the medical literature, he found that similar disease had occurred in Poitou, France, and had been described by François Citois in 1617. The colic of Poitou only visited people who drank Rhenish or Moselle wines that had been treated with litharge (lead monoxide) to improve the flavor. Baker first questioned whether acid itself could cause this disease, but he noted that the Turks at that time consumed large quantities of acid sherbet with no ill effects, and also that jockeys who drank vinegar in order to lose weight did not contract the disease. He also observed the inhabitants of the Bahamas who drank a great deal of punch made with limes; they likewise seemed well. He then experimented with a dog, giving it 3½ ounces of very strong vinegar. The dog died, but there was no inflammation of his organs, except his lungs, which were presumably irritated by the inhalation of the strong vinegar. He noted also that the physician Brannerus had killed a dog with an ounce of powder of litharge dissolved and boiled in vinegar (producing lead acetate). The effects of the chemical were evident principally in the stomach, intestines, urinary bladder, and the rest of the abdominal viscera.

Baker concluded that the people of Devonshire had developed the constipation and paralytic weakness of lead poisoning, some even losing their sanity. The answer to the riddle was the widespread use of lead in the Devonshire apple presses to close the interstices between the grinding stones. This is a classic epidemiological study on the effects of a metal, lead, used in the preparation of a foodstuff, cider. Lead poisoning can still happen, but lead poisoning from food is an extremely rare occurrence in the western world.

In recent years in the United States and Canada there has been considerable interest in lead poisoning, particularly in children. Severe lead poisoning is almost always associated with the licking of old paint or newsprint or dirt—children will try to eat almost anything. It is also possible to get lead poisoning from dishes or jugs that have been treated with lead. There has been some concern about the possibility of lead in baby foods, but as far as we know there is considerably less in baby foods than a few years ago.

Another metallic poison that may contaminate food is mercury. In classical mercury poisoning with large amounts of the metal, there is clumsiness and fumbling in the execution of all movements, especially with the eyes closed. The gait is wide-based and uncertain; the feet hit the ground with undue force. The movements of the upper limb are slow and clumsy, and fine movements are carried out with great difficulty. Sufferers cannot speak properly or articulate clearly, and in some situations they cannot speak at all. In some countries mercurial dressings have been used on seeds to protect them against fungi, although not in North America. But in Iraq in 1972, as mentioned earlier, more than 3000 people died after eating seed grain that had been treated with mercury. Symptoms usually appear within four to six weeks of eating bread made from wheat contaminated with mercury salts.

The well-known Minimata Disease occurred in 1953 among poor fishermen and their families living along Minimata Bay in Japan. The clinical features of Minimata Disease include numbness in the extremities and around the mouth, accompanied by slurred speech. Most victims complained of deafness and disturbances of vision, the latter being associated with damage to the visual fields. In some cases insomnia was a striking feature, and acute depression was apparent. The death rate reached 40 per cent and it took six years of investigation before the cause was isolated: A factory discharging its effluent into Minimata Bay. This factory made acetaldehyde and vinyl chloride, using mercuric chloride as a catalyst; methyl mercury was an unsuspected by-product, contaminating fish and other edible seafood in Minimata Bay.

Methyl mercury is unfortunately a common contaminant of rivers, streams, and lakes, especially by industries such as paper mills and chlorine manufacturers. In general, mercury in food is not a threat in North America, except possibly to people who eat enormous quantities of fish every day.

A Final Word on Additives

In general it is clear that food additives add greatly to the appearance, flavor, and keeping qualities of foods. Public concern about the chemicals they consume is a good thing, and government agencies and manufacturers are well aware of this concern. But the public and the news media should be concerned only with facts, and we must maintain a sense of proportion. No one is trying deliberately to poison the people of North America by knowingly putting toxicants in their food.

TABLE 3:5

SOME WIDELY USED FOOD ADDITIVES

Additive	Function
Monosodium glutamate	Flavor enhancer
Mustard	Flavor
Black pepper	Flavor
Hydrolyzed vegetable protein	Stabilizer (thickener)
Acacia	Stabilizer (thickener)
Modified starch	Stabilizer (thickener)
Yeasts	Leavening
Monocalcium phosphate	Leavening
Sodium aluminum phosphate	Leavening
Sodium acid phosphate	Leavening
Sodium carbonate	Leavening, acidity control
Calcium carbonate	Leavening, acidity control
Dicalcium phosphate	Leavening, acidity control
Disodium phosphate	Leavening, acidity control
Sodium bicarbonate	Acidity control
Hydrogen chloride	Acidity control
Citric acid	Acidity control
Sulfuric acid	Acidity control
Sodium citrate	Acidity control
Sodium hydroxide	Acidity control
Acetic acid	Acidity control
Phosphoric acid	Acidity control
Calcium oxide	Acidity control
Lecithin	Emulsifier
Mono and diglycerides	Emulsifiers
Sulfur dioxide	Preservative
Calcium chloride	Firming agent
Calcium sulfate	Processing aid
Carbon dioxide	Effervescent
Sodium tripolyphosphate	Curing humectant
Caramel	Color

Source: Richard L. Hall, 1973. Food additives, Nutrition Today. (4):20–28. Reproduced by permission of Nutrition Today. ªConsumed annually in amounts of 9 pounds per day.
Source: Packard, V. S. (1976) Processed Foods and The Consumer. University of Minnesota Press. Minneapolis.

4.

Natural Poisons in Foods

It is ironic, in this age of concern over food additives, that most people are unaware of the equally, if not more grave danger from poisons occurring naturally in food. In the United States the Delaney Clause of the Food and Drug Act prohibits any substance that is found to cause cancer when ingested by humans or animals *in any dosage* from being added to foods in any amount. Yet carcinogens or suspected carcinogens that occur naturally are not restricted in any way. So it is that aflatoxins, a potent carcinogen, are often found in peanuts in very low concentrations. Even milk contains aflatoxins in very low concentrations. In general we have to assume that even this severe carcinogen in very low concentrations is not harmful.

If we subscribe to the Delaney philosophy, a hard look at a typical dinner menu would give pause for thought. A paper on the subject was written a few years ago by Dr. Richard L. Hall, who in 1976 was named the chemist of the year for the Maryland Branch of the American Chemical Society.

The "Dangers" in a Good Meal

The menu: Relish tray—carrots, radishes, onions, olives
Dinner rolls
Melon crescents wrapped in ham

Shrimp Newburg with watercress garnish
Broccoli with hollandaise sauce
Parsleyed new potatoes
Cheese and fruit

Let's start with the relish tray. We've all been told that carrots are very good for us—we know that from carrots we get carotene, the precursor of vitamin A. What most of us don't know, however, is that carrots contain caratotoxin, a nerve poison that would make many a toxicologist blanch. Carrots also contain myristicin, a hallucinogen also found in nutmeg and other foodstuffs, as well as some other substances, probably isoflavones, that have an estrogenic effect. Better pass on the carrots.

Radishes contain goitrogens, chemicals that produce goiters by interfering with the body's utilization of iodine. About 50g of radishes would be expected to have a noticeable influence on iodine metabolism. So we shouldn't eat the radishes. And for those who like to terrify themselves with chemical names, here are two substances found in radishes: 4 methyl-thio-3 butanyl, glucosinolate; and 3-indolylmethyl glucosmolate (or glucobrassicin). In onions there is a mixture of methyl, propyl, isopropyl, 1-propenyl, and allyl disulphides and trisulphides, which also show antithyroid or goitrogenic activity. Clearly we should not eat radishes or onions.

Olives, of course, have been soaked in dilute lye—sodium or potassium hydroxide—which helps to remove the bitter flavor. They are then washed and soaked in brine, so obviously they contain far too much sodium. They also contain tannins, as well as low levels of benzo(a)pyrene, a potent carcinogen. Under the Delaney Clause, no carcinogen is permitted. We should, therefore, dispose of the olives, and that takes care of the relish tray.

Now to the melon slices wrapped in ham. Of course, the ham has been smoked, and if it has been naturally smoked it contains at least one carcinogen, again our old acquaintance, benzo(a)pyrene. Furthermore, ham has been treated with sodium nitrate and sodium nitrite, about which, under the Delaney Clause, there are grave doubts. We are now left with naked melon crescents.

Let's leave the melon for now and take a look at the shrimp Newburg. Shrimps are a good source of many minerals. They also contain between 40 and 170 or more parts per million of arsenic, much more than we could tolerate or than the Food and Drug law would allow, using the 100-fold safety factor. Shrimps also contain a lot of iodine, which is toxic at very high levels. And they are one of the richest sources of copper; 200 parts per million of copper in the diet is probably the maximum "no effect" level in humans, and shrimps may contain twice that. Too bad about the shrimps. Now, what about the Newburg sauce?

This sauce consists of lobster, butter, brandy, flour, and fish stock. An important constituent of butter is vitamin A, and we know that in certain animal experiments a deficiency or an excess of vitamin A has been teratogenic. In other words, it has produced deformities of the fetus in animals, so we are naturally worried about the vitamin A question, not to mention the dangers of saturated fatty acids. Then, the brandy. We know that alcohol may be dangerous, and it contains fusel oil, which produces hangovers. Lobster suffers from the same drawbacks as shrimp. Without the lobster and butter and brandy, the Newburg sauce is unattractive, to say the least.

Surely potatoes would be a safe bet! But wait—potatoes are members of the nightshade family, most of which contain an alkaloid called solanine, which inhibits cholinesterase. This means that it interferes with the transmission of nerve impulses, in the same way as nerve gases do. The solanine is near the skin of the potato, with the vitamin C, and there is more in new potatoes than in old ones. We aren't certain what the solanine safety factor is in new potatoes, so if anybody were to feel somewhat drowsy or almost paralyzed or have difficulty in breathing after eating new potatoes, it may have been solanine at work. Potato poisoning can happen.

And as for parsley—this ubiquitous garnish contains psoralen, which makes the skin sensitive to light. If we eat enough parsley or rub it on the skin, it may produce an unusual sensitivity to sunlight in either severe sunburn or later tanning. It also contains myristicin. The other garnish, watercress, contains not only a goitrogen, but also an antivitamin that renders thiamine hydrochloride, or vitamin B_1, ineffective.

Broccoli contains five goitrogens, all of them inhibiting our utilization of iodine, so obviously we should view broccoli with concern. Hollandaise sauce is made with egg yolk and butter and lemon juice. We've already looked at the risks involved in eating butter. Leaving aside the worry about cholesterol in egg yolk, we still know that it's loaded with vitamins A and D, excesses of which may be harmful. Lemon juice contains a host of harmful substances, citral for one. Citral may damage the lining of the circulatory system if it is given to animals, and it also counteracts the good effects of vitamin A. Lemon juice also contains synephrine, which increases the blood pressure, and isopimpinellin, which also renders the skin sensitive to light, like the action of psoralen in parsley. Obviously the hollandaise sauce is questionable.

As for the wine, many people look on alcohol as a poison, but in addition it may also contain pressor amines, which increase the blood pressure.

We have mentioned previously a substance called synephrine, one of a group of chemicals, pressor amines, that increase blood pressure. In most people a diet containing pressor amines has no effect, because our bodies contain an enzyme system called monoamine oxidase, which rapidly and effectively changes these amines into fragments we can excrete. Some people, however, have reduced monoamine oxidase capacity, particularly if they have been taking certain antidepressant drugs. In such cases pressor amines may be harmful.

At the end of this meal, we could eat cheese, but we should remember that cheese, too, contains pressor amines. So do bananas and avocados. Apples are very nutritious, but they're not free of toxic chemicals. One of them is phlorizin, which may produce glucosuria—glucose in the urine. The consequence of eating too many apples might be a degree of sugar in the urine that would frighten our insurance agents.

More bad news: coffee is a rich source of tannin and caffeine, both dangerous substances. And as coffee is a roasted product, it contains a carcinogen. Tea contains not only tannin, but fluorine. We must remember that while some fluorine is useful, in eight to 10 parts per million in the diet it can lead to skeletal fluorosis, with pain, stiffness, and excessive calcification.

What's left of the meal? Melon crescents, a pastry roll, and mineral water. Melons don't contain much except water, but you can't even count on that to be safe.

A Sense of Balance

This depressing analysis of a typical dinner menu illustrates an important point: We must maintain a sense of balance about poisons, additives, and foods. I feel, as do many others, that we have been worrying about the wrong things. We have become obsessed with additives, and we have forgotten that there are natural poisons in our foods that may occur in fairly high concentrations. The foods in our sample menu are not danger-ous as part of a balanced diet. They are nutritious and they are safe. The fact that they contain chemicals does not necessarily make them poisonous, for the potentially dangerous chemicals occur in very low concentrations. As we have said before, dosage is the key. If a poison or drug is present in a very small or low concentration, it does not exert a harmful effect.

This same principle applies to the many other poisons that are currently being bandied about in the press. At the time of writing there is great excitement in Toronto about dioxin in the water supply. Dioxins are extremely poisonous, but as they have appeared in the water supplies in very low concentrations, it is extremely doubtful that they are having a deleterious effect. The good that has come for the public from the furor is that all efforts will now be made to limit the manufacture of substances that contain dioxins or to change the manufacturing process so that little or no dioxin is produced. There's no reason to assume that amounts presently consumed are harmful, but there's no reason to keep consuming more dioxins, either. The human body is remarkably efficient in coping with poisons in very low concentrations. Although we're not about to encourage the development of poisons or the use of them, we strongly urge a sense of balance and a sense of proportion about them.

Toxicity of Pure Foods

Having illustrated that there are natural poisons, and having pointed out examples of the poisonous substances present in all foods that we eat every day, let's look at the possible toxic effects of pure foods. In fact, many pure foods can be harmful if eaten exclusively and in large amounts.

Some years ago the late Professor E. M. Boyd, Professor emeritus of Pharmacology, Queen's University, Kingston, Ontario, produced a book, edited by his son, Dr. Carl Boyd, called *The Toxicity of Pure Foods*. Their studies showed that a large amount of *any* pure food can kill laboratory animals. Dr. Boyd pointed out that toxic dose varies with body weight. For example, a dose of 25g of sucrose—common sugar—per kg of body weight is a fatal dose for albino rats. An equivalent dose for a child of 22 pounds would be ½ pound of candy. The point is that even pure foods may be dangerous. And because the toxic dose varies with body weight, a child is more likely than an adult to consume a lethal dose.

Other examples of pure foods that can kill laboratory animals if fed in excessive amounts: glucose, starch, cotton-seed oil, corn oil, egg white powder, high protein diets, distilled water, and sodium chloride. No doubt if they were eaten in the same amounts relative to body weight, they would kill people too.

Herbal Smokes and Teas

The past few years have seen a considerable increase in the medical and non-medical use of various herbal products, including cigarets, smoking mixtures, teas, and capsules. These substances are often recognized as natural drugs, many of them containing psychoactive substances, and they are apparently easily obtainable. As far as we know there are at least 192 herbs commercially available for use as smoking substances. They are combined in many types of mixtures, including yerba santa, rosemary, thyme, mullein, and spearmint; some of these mixtures contain various herbs that are said to fuel the effects of marijuana.

One 30-year-old man was brought into the hospital in a confused state. His pupils were dilated and reacted minimally to light. His mouth and throat were dry, his speech slurred and hesitant. He had blurred vision, couldn't walk properly, and had difficulty concentrating. He had been smoking a non-tobacco smoking substitute called Mint Bidis, which contain enormous quantities of atropine and scopolomine, hardly health-promoting drugs. Another type of cigaret from India, the Hare Rama Bidis, contained enormous levels of nicotine, much more than in American cigarets.

A number of herbal teas are widely available. There are at least 396 distinct herbs and spices commercially available that are used in blends as herbal teas. Many of them contain psychoactive agents. For instance, there is a case description of a 29-year-old man who came to the hospital complaining of a chronic intoxicated feeling, accompanied by loss of appetite and diarrhea. He was extremely emaciated, his skin was yellow, and he had yellow banding on the finger and toenails. He also had rashes and other dermatoses. He had difficulty in focusing, his hearing was poor, and he could not move his muscles properly. What he had been drinking was kava kava tea, made from the crushed roots of the kava plant (Piper meristicum), a shrub found in the South Pacific and used in religious ceremonies, allegedly to delay and reduce fatigue. It is not recommended for its health-promoting qualities.

Another interesting case is that of a 37-year-old woman at a party who drank a tea made from two ground nutmegs in a glass of warm water. After drinking it she experienced a warm feeling, slight nausea, sweating, dryness in the mouth and throat, and an intoxicated, drowsy feeling. When she was examined by her physician 12 hours later, she had flushed skin, rapid pulse, and incoherent speech, and she was dizzy. Her vision was disturbed, she had hallucinations: "Her face was laughing at her," monsters in the bed were trying to engulf her. These symptoms, which diminished over a period of 24 hours, were the effects of myristicin, which causes central nervous system depression.

Another man drank some Jimson weed tea *(Datura stramonium)*. This very poisonous plant contains large amounts of atropine and scopolomine. The man had hallucinations of demons, animals, and voodoo people chasing him. He became disoriented, wandering in the woods for several hours, running barefoot over nettles and harsh brush and lacerating his feet. He felt terrible for many days following this incident.

Many herbal handbooks suggest that herbal teas be combined with herb capsules. We do not know what all these herb capsules do, but we do know of one 30-year-old man who came to the hospital complaining of nervousness, insomnia, and trembling. He was a strict vegetarian and avoided the use of alcohol, cigarets, and coffee as well as other psychoactive drugs. Recently, however, he had been taking capsules called Gotu Kola, because he had heard that they were good for the brain. When he took them he had an increase in energy, diminished appetite, and elevation of mood. He most regrettably did not experience the enhancement of intellectual performance claimed by the advertisement. Gotu Kola is ground kola nut, a well-known stimulant.

A number of teas are used as diuretics—buchu, quack grass, and common dandelion among them. They are not particularly good diuretics. Other diuretic substances are juniper berries, which can irritate the gastrointestinal tract, and shave grass or horsetail, both of which contain nicotine and thiaminase. When horses and other grazing animals eat these plants they may experience loss of appetite, excitement, loss of muscular control, diarrhea, difficulty in breathing, convulsions, even death. Many herbal teas are violent purgatives; teas containing buckthorn and senna leaves have caused very serious diarrhea. Dockroot and aloe leaves can also be very strong. Veterinarians use aloes for constipation in elephants and cattle.

Many of these substances sold in health-food stores are not clearly identified, and many of them are contaminated by other substances that may have harmful effects. Some may cause allergic reactions. Chamomile tea, for example, is usually considered harmless, but it may cause severe dermatitis, epileptic shock, and hypersensitivity reactions in people who are allergic to ragweed, asters, and chrysanthemums. These people may also become sick from teas made from goldenrod, marigold, and yarrow. Licorice root in large amounts can cause sodium and water retention, a lack of potassium, high blood pressure, and even heart failure and heart stoppage. Sassafrass root, which contains safrole, which causes liver damage, is carcinogenic in animals.

The Chinese have used ginseng as a herbal remedy without harm for many years, although it contains small amounts of estrogens and has been reported to cause swollen and painful breasts. The catch is that we don't know whether all the substances sold as ginseng are really ginseng. Sometimes marigold root, which contains a poison, and snakeroot, which contains reserpine, are sold as ginseng.

Other substances that could cause trouble are mistletoe leaves, which may cause severe gastroenteritis, contraction of smooth muscle, shock, and cardiac arrest. The berries of the pokeweed or inkberry are poisonous, and children have been killed by them. We also know that many fruit seeds contain amygdalin, which liberates hydrogen cyanide, a severe poison, in the body when eaten. Children have been poisoned and some have died after eating such seeds, which include apricot pits, bitter almonds, cherry and peach pits, and pear, apple, and plum seeds. We know that adults have been poisoned by drinking milkshakes that included apricot kernels. In tropical countries the consumption of cassava that has not been properly treated may produce goiter, nervous symptoms, and double vision because of chronic cyanide intoxication.

The lesson in all this is to be very careful in buying teas and smokes from health-food stores; who knows what you are buying or what you will be smoking, using, or infusing. Many of these herbal remedies may be extremely harmful. It is ironic that people who do not believe in doctors or in scientific medicine have now adopted the witchcraft inherent in many of these herbal remedies. By and large, medical science has investigated herbal remedies and uses them as medicaments if they are effective. Nowadays we prefer to use the pure chemical substance refined from plants so that we know the exact chemical composition and dosage. Not all herbal remedies are harmful, but it's wise to steer clear of them unless you know what you're doing. Most people selling these substances in health-food stores have no medical or scientific training. They don't know what they are selling or what these products will do.

There has, of course, grown up in Europe and North America a group of herbalists who know a great deal about herbal remedies and who also know the dangers of such remedies. These are not the people who sell dangerous substances.

Some Exotic Poisonous Foods

In Canada an interesting report, *Poison Control Statistics,* is issued every year by Dr. E. Napke of the Department of National Health and Welfare. These statistics show that drugs of various types account for about half of all poisonings, and non-drugs the other half. Of the drugs, the commonest poisons are Aspirin or other acetylsalicylic acid products, Valium, iron tablets, acetaminophen, Ex-Lax (a purgative), Dalmane (a sleeping pill), Librium, Gravol, and Mandrax (a sleeping pill). Half of the toxic doses of drugs are taken by children under the age of four—small children will eat almost anything.

In the non-drug group, plants are responsible for 9.5 per cent of poisonings, and of course many small children are poisoned by cosmetics, pesticides, petroleum hydrocarbons, cleaning and polishing agents, and chemical gases and vapors. Toddlers will also eat fertilizers, glues, and adhesives. Out of the 60,712 cases of poisonings in 1976, 2192 poisonings were by plants and 1142 were by substances ingested because they were thought to be food. Ordinary food poisoning accounted for 1145 poisonings; such food poisoning is discussed in later chapters.

Among the hazards to children are some common houseplants. A plant called daphne, particularly *Daphne mezereum,* has toxic berries. *Dieffenbachia picta,* also called dumb cane, is poisonous. At Christmastime there are quite a few cases of poisoning by holly, which contains the toxin ilicin, causing vomiting, diarrhea, and deep or mild narcosis. There are many species of holly used as ornamental shrubs in North America.

All types of mistletoe are highly toxic, and every year a few children in North America die after eating it. Poinsettia is also poisonous, as is Jerusalem cherry, a member of the night-shade *(Solanum)* family. Solanum poisoning results in burning in the mouth and throat, nausea, weakness, dizziness, and convulsions. These plants also contain atropine and may some-times develop toxic concentrations of nitrates. Belladonna or deadly nightshade, *Atropa belladonna,* is a perennial herb that is imported from Europe as an ornamental plant. As few as three of its attractive black berries can be fatal. Among the drugs found in deadly nightshade are hyoscyamine, atropine, scopolamine, and a large number of similar drugs, all of which are poisonous.

Common rhubarb may be poisonous, as the leaf contains a great deal of oxalic acid. There are also a number of cases of poisoning by sweet peas. The wild sweet pea is sometimes mistaken for related edible plants. Both it and the cultivated sweet pea, *Lathyrus odoratus,* contain an alkaloid in the stem that causes paralysis.

A significant number of poisonings occur from mushroom species, as it is often difficult to distinguish between poisonous and edible mushrooms. For instance, there are something like 30 species of *Amanita* mushrooms in North America, some edible, others deadly. *Amanita phalloides* is the most danger-ous. In France *Amanita* poisoning is so common that anti-*Amanita* serum is required by law to be stocked so as to be available to all physicians. The false morel, *Helvella esculenta,* looks very much like the edible morel, but it is poisonous when grown in some soils and not in others. There are, of course, many other types of poisonous mushrooms. Commercially raised mushrooms that are widely available in North America and Europe are obviously not dangerous. The difficulty with mush-rooms comes when people pick their own in the wild. "Natu-ral" mushrooms sometimes have considerable surprises in store for the people who eat them.

Some Poisonous Animals

To people largely reared on domestic animals, it may come as a surprise that there are animals that are toxic to humans. It is difficult to determine, but scientists have concluded that poisonous animals apparently produce much more sickness and death than do poisonous plants. There is a large list of poisonous animals, but we will mention only the relatively common ones.

Flagellates are small, one-celled creatures that can grow in mollusks and other marine animals and may cause poisoning. Some sea anemones, starfish, and sea urchins may be poisonous. Sea cucumbers have been said to be poisonous.

Many mollusks are poisonous, and something like 10 million metric tons of marine mollusks are annually consumed on the world market. Sometimes they are rendered poisonous by dinoflagellate toxins. The mollusks themselves are not harmed when they eat these microscopic creatures, but the poisons are stored in the digestive glands, gills, or siphons of the mollusks. Vertebrates—people or fish—who eat them are poisoned. Sometimes there are massive fish kills associated with red ocean water—a "red tide" produced by dinoflagellates in the water. Poisoning from dinoflaglellates starts with a tingling or burning of the lips, gums, tongue, and face, gradually spreading to other parts of the body, which develop numbness. There is weakness, dizziness, aching joints, excessive saliva production, tremendous thirst, difficulty in swallowing, and difficult muscle movement. Muscle paralysis may increase and death may result. The treatment consists of stomach washouts and purgatives; there is no specific antidote available. Heat does not destroy this toxin, and boiling may not dissolve all of it into the broth. Flagellates proliferate during the warm months in North America, May to September, and in some places March to November, and that is why we avoid eating oysters and other mollusks at that time of year.

In Japan people are very often poisoned by octopus or squid; the nature of the toxin is not known. Some edible crabs are poisonous at certain times. Horseshoe crabs from Asia, for example, are periodically toxic and not always sold. There is no treatment for poisoning by these crabs. Sometimes people are poisoned by the flesh of sharks, particularly the liver. Moray eels living in tropical areas may also cause poisoning.

There are many tropical fish that become poisonous because they have fed on poisonous marine organisms. The trigger fish and parrot fish are poisonous during most of the year, the moon fish and goat fish only part of the year. Barracuda, mackerel, snapper, and sea bass are poisonous only at certain times and in certain places; in some areas they are always safe to eat. There are at least 300 species that have been reported to cause poisoning. In some tropical countries morbidity may reach 50 per cent of the population in limited areas. Poisoning by fish is particularly common in Hawaii. There are a number of fish, including tuna, bonito, mackerel, and skipjack, that become toxic when exposed to warm temperatures.

Most animal toxins are not detectable by the usual smell of decomposition. There are countless folk tales about how to distinguish the toxic from the non-toxic, but these are unreliable. The flesh may have a sharp, peppery taste. Symptoms include headaches, dizziness, throbbing of the large leg muscles, dryness of the mouth, heart palpitation, difficulty in swallowing, nausea, vomiting, diarrhea, and abdominal pain. Some people develop large, intensely itchy welts. There may be death from shock.

A type of poisoning called ciguatera poisoning results from eating different types of unrelated fish that are ecologically associated in narrow regions with coral reefs. Symptoms of acute poisoning start 30 minutes to four hours after ingestion—numbness and tingling of the face and lips, spreading to the fingers and toes, followed by nausea, vomiting, diarrhea, malaise, abdominal pain, dizziness, and muscular weakness. In very severe poisoning symptoms progress to foaming at the mouth, difficulty in breathing, muscular paralysis, and convulsions. Death may occur from convulsions or respiratory arrest within one to 24 hours. If the victim recovers from the immediate symptoms, muscular weakness and the tingling of the face, lips, and mouth may persist for weeks. More than 300 species of fish have been incriminated in ciguatera poisoning, all in warm seas ranging from Japan to India, East Africa, the Red Sea, Polynesia, the Marshall Islands, and Hawaii.

In the far north, if anybody were so unwise as to eat sled dogs, they might be poisoned by the high vitamin A content of the livers. Seal and polar bear livers are equally toxic. Symptoms of vitamin A poisoning include headaches, nausea, vomiting, diarrhea, abdominal pain, dizziness, drowsiness, irritability, collapse, light sensitivity, and convulsions. Death does not usually occur.

A Serious Natural Carcinogen: The Aflatoxins

One of the most potent carcinogens known is a naturally occurring poison—aflatoxins, which are produced in certain fungi. This group of toxins was first recognized in 1960 with a serious outbreak of disease in turkey flocks in the south and east of England. In the first series of outbreaks more than 100,000 birds died. The disease was also reported in ducklings and chickens. Although the toxic agent was unknown, the obvious target of suspicion was the animals' feed. In due course the finger was pointed at certain types of peanut meal coming from Brazil, but researchers subsequently found aflatoxins occurred in at least 14 peanut-producing countries in widely scattered geographic areas. And they were not confined to peanuts; they have been found in oil seeds such as cottonseed; in soybeans, corn, rice, wheat, millet, barley, sorghum, beans, peas, cassava, and yams. Even now we don't know how widely these substances are distributed.

It was found that the toxins were associated with the growth of a fungus identified as *Aspergillus flavus,* which grows particularly well in conditions of high relative humidity and relatively high temperature, about 30°C—conditions common in the tropics. Aflatoxin production can occur before most harvest drying reduces moisture content below a critical level. If peanuts are dried very rapidly after harvesting, and kept dry, the fungus does not grow effectively.

Every effort is made in North America to find and destroy crops with high aflatoxin content. Even so, these natural carcinogens are found in peanut butter in very low concentrations, as well as in other foods. Aflatoxin acts mainly on the liver, producing acute destruction, hemorrhage, and chronic fibrosis. Many believe that the high rate of primary carcinoma of the liver in Africa is due to the chronic toxic effect of aflatoxins over a long period of time.

There are many other toxins produced by fungi, including fungi in rice and fungi in grain in the Soviet Union. The best known of these is ergot, from grains infested with the mold, *Clavicepts purpurea*. In the Middle Ages the toxic symptoms were called St. Anthony's Fire; diarrhea and vomiting, followed by headaches, dizziness, strange feelings in the extremities, convulsions, and occasionally gangrene of the toes, fingers, nose and ears. This peripheral gangrene is due to arterial spasm and slow blood flow in the arteries and the formation of clots. Ergot poisoning in the past has occurred in epidemic form. It may also occur after repeated administration intended to produce abortion.

A Sense of Proportion

This discussion is not intended to terrify the public about the hidden dangers in food. If we eat a good mixed diet from sound sources, it is highly improbable that we will be poisoned by our foods. On the other hand, if governmental agencies relax in monitoring our foods, we could again be poisoned by substances such as aflatoxins. This situation exists in many Third World countries, where there is not only a lack of food, but where food is not properly stored. Nuts and grain crops are harvested in warm, moist weather and they are not stored in such a way as to dry them out quickly, resulting in a great deal of preventable disease from fungal intoxication.

We should also point out that, even in North America, if foods, particularly grains and legumes, are produced in a natural way and allowed to dry in a natural way, they may cause widespread disease. Human beings use their intelligence to improve upon nature; it is knowledge of fungal growth that has made it possible to produce legumes and grains with very low concentrations of aflatoxins and other toxins of fungal origin.

5.

Pesticides and Other Chemicals

Since the beginnings of agriculture about 8000 years ago, humans have had to share their food production with many other creatures, who learned to like the things we planted. Micro-organisms, insects, birds, rodents, and other animals compete fiercely for a share of the harvest. Plants, too, compete for a share of the agricultural land, even to the point of choking out cultivated crops. Table 5:1 shows the percentage of crops that would be lost to all these competitors if we did not intervene.

Before this century, there was little that could be done to protect crops. Scarecrows and traps helped discourage the larger pests; a sharp hoe and a lot of elbow grease kept weeds at bay. A few pesticides were available; arsenic was used on the Colorado potato beetle, Paris green on a wide range of insects. Copper and mercury compounds were used for disease control, although we now know that mercury is dangerous to humans.

Also in use were two insecticides derived from plants: Rotenone, from the roots of a South American plant; and pyrethrin, from the flowers of a small Asian chrysanthemum. Both are still popular with organic gardeners as they are non-toxic to humans and animals and are biodegradable, leaving no toxic residue. Sulfur was also used until recently to control insects and mites on plants. By the beginning of World War II, there were only about 30 pesticides in use.

The development of pesticides—including insecticides,

TABLE 5:1

PERCENTAGE OF LOSSES IN MAJOR
AGRICULTURAL CROPS ON WORLD BASIS DUE TO
INSECTS, DISEASES, AND WEEDS[a]

Crop	Insects	Diseases	Weeds	Total
Wheat	5	9	10	24
Oats	8	9	10	27
Barley	4	8	9	23
Rye	2	3	10	15
Rice	27	9	11	46
Millets and sorghums	10	11	18	38
Maize (corn)	12	9	13	35
Potatoes	5	22	4	32
Sugar cane	20	19	16	55
Citrus fruit	8	9	4	22
Grapes	3	23	10	37
Oil crops	11	10	11	32
Vegetables	9	10	9	28

[a]After Cramer (1967). Estimates are based on various production (quatitative) tables from Cramer and are rounded to whole numbers. Thus "Total" figures may not equal the sum of the 3 preceding columns.
Source: McEwen F. L. and Stephenson G. R. (1979). The Use and Significance of Pesticides in The Environment. John Wiley and Sons. New York.

herbicides, and fungicides—in the last 40 years has coincided with an enormous growth in human populations, because it became increasingly important to improve and increase food production. This technology, which began in the western world, has now spread around the globe—many small farmers in Asia, Africa, and South America are now using various pesticides to control fungal, bacterial, and insect predators that destroy their crops. It is important to realize that this chemical world that has burgeoned since 1939 is a world we have made, of necessity. It is the world in which we live, and it is a world from which there is no escape. The best we can do is to develop those pesticides that will be as effective as possible on the pests for which they are required. A great deal of scientific research is needed to develop pesticides that will not be poisonous to humans or to other creatures. This, of course, is a difficult task, but considerable progress has been made during the last ten years, particularly since we have become conscious of the fact that pesticides are a somewhat mixed blessing.

DDT (dichloro-diphenyl-trichloroethane) was first synthesized in 1874, but its insecticidal properties were discovered much later by a researcher named Müller, who was searching for a substance to control clothes moths. The first major use of DDT was to control lice in World War II, when in 1943 it eliminated an outbreak of typhus in Naples, saving the U.S. Army from a disease that in previous campaigns had killed many people. DDT was then used against many vectors, including the mosquito and rat flea. In Sardinia it was so effective against malaria-carrying mosquitoes that its use was proposed in an attempt at global eradication of malaria in 1955. But as so often happens in nature, the mosquitoes developed a resistance to the chemical. DDT was also extremely useful in agriculture, where its use resulted in considerable increases in crop yields.

The other important use of pesticides is in weed control. Herbicides such as 2,4-D and atrazene are special herbicides that help in the mechanization of crop production, and there are now countless specific herbicides that can be used on a wide variety of crops, destroying weeds without harming cultivated plants. There are also products for bird control, fish control, rodent control, and even nematode control.

Of course, the use of many of the pesticides has produced ecological imbalances, in some cases with disastrous results. Massive fish kills resulted from DDT spraying for spruce budworm control in New Brunswick, and there have been other reports of fish mortality. Rachel Carson's book, *Silent Spring,* published in 1962, brought to the notice of the public some of the dangers of pesticides to bird and animal life and to people. DDT was not the only pesticide found in various living creatures. There is no doubt that several pesticides have adversely affected wildlife. Others have caused considerable health risks among workers, particularly the organophosphates and organochlorides. The contaminants of certain pesticides are suspected of having teratogenic or mutagenic effects; "teratogenic" means causing deformed fetuses, and "mutagenic" means the genetic change of cells. There is no doubt that there should be more controls on pesticides, but they are so useful in increasing food production that we cannot do without them.

There are many intelligent, thoughtful people who are opposed to all pesticides. But how do we convince the rest of the people in the world that they will have to be satisfied with half the amount of food now being produced? How can today's world population face the prospect of only half or a quarter of the food presently available to them? Quite clearly, for the future survival of the world it would be much better if there were only one billion people in it, but the fact is that there are 4.6 billion people, and their numbers are increasing by approximately 80 million each year. It is for these people that the use of pesticides, and chemical fertilizers, is necessary.

Many of our best food crops are unable to compete in the natural environment without considerable supplements of nutrients and moisture and protection from pests. The crops that form the basis of our food supply have been bred for high yields and eye appeal rather than for survival under adverse conditions. As a matter of fact, some of the new types of rice and wheat *need* pesticides to survive at all.

Furthermore, modern insecticides control the spread of disease by killing the insect vectors: Mosquitoes that carry malaria and yellow fever; the tsetse fly in Africa and kissing bugs in South America that transmit trypanosomiasis; the rat flea, which carries plague; and the louse, which carries epidemic typhus. Pesticides have made it possible for many people to survive, particularly in the tropics. In Canada and the United States, pesticides have been used to kill mosquitoes carrying St. Louis encephalitis.

The fact that pesticides are poisonous is stimulating further research to make pesticides that are not only less poisonous, but also biodegradable. And we have as yet only begun to investigate biological controls such as companion planting and beneficial predators.

Alternatives to Pesticides

It does not seem probable that the world can easily survive the heavy load of potent chemicals now being placed upon the agricultural soil. We must develop ecologically sound methods of controlling insects and other pests that will not be harmful to the total environment—a very difficult task, but one that must be squarely faced. We need methods of control that are more in balance with nature. There are two key points to remember. First, there are about one million known species of insects, most of them harmless, many beneficial. Most insecticides are nonspecific—they kill everything. Second, agriculture is, in fact, an artificial situation in nature, and the increased foodstuffs it has produced have encouraged the growth and development of the very insects who eat these foods.

A fascinating example of the use and abuse of insecticide is the story of the cotton boll weevil. This insect first came to Texas from Mexico in 1892. It survives during the winter in the plants and debris around the cotton fields. Before DDT the trash around the cotton fields was removed and destroyed, thus at least keeping the insects somewhat under control. In the 1920s arsenic poisons were used, but they obviously were inadequate in controlling the weevil. After World War II everyone saw DDT as the ultimate answer to the weevil problem, and tons of it were dumped on the cotton fields, while at the same time cultivation practices deteriorated. What happened next was that DDT produced boll weevils that were resistant to this chemical. Back they came into the fields in droves. Other insecticides were brought into the battle, and the struggle is still going on. To complicate matters, in certain areas the place of the boll weevil was taken by the tobacco budworm. It is now the most troublesome pest in cotton, and it is resistant to most insecticides. This story is but one example of an imbalance produced by the unwise application of pesticides. Current control of the tobacco budworm and the boll weevil in cotton fields is much more complicated as a result of the development of insecticides. In 1969 large areas in Texas and in northern Mexico no longer produced cotton.

What are the solutions to this problem? There are a number of suggested alternatives, the first being that we reduce as much as possible the number of chemicals used on the land, and instead use other insects to control destructive ones. We know, for instance, that the lacewing and the ladybug eat aphids. We know that predator insects such as parasitic wasps kill certain plant-eating caterpillars. There is a company in California that breeds wasps which then prey on the red scale insect that destroys citrus fruits.

Another interesting advance is the synthesis of pheromones, chemical substances that are secreted by insects and animals to attract the opposite sex. Some insects can be controlled by the proper use of pheromones. Another answer to insect control is to irradiate the males of the species, sterilizing them. In the future there will have to be a judicious combination of the wise use of insecticides combined with biological controls to protect our food supply. In the meantime, it would be helpful to know what we are dealing with and what risks are entailed.

Types of Insecticide

The major types of insecticide are:

1. *minerals*—fuel oil, kerosene, sulfur, and borax—some of the oldest insecticides, still widely used.
2. *botanicals*—pyrethrin and rotenone, in use before 1900 and still favorites because they leave no toxic residue. Synthetic pyrethroids can be manufactured and standardized in quantity.
3. *chlorinated hydrocarbons*—DDT, lindane, and chlordane were the most widely used insecticides from the 1940s through the 1960s. However, problems of resistance and environmental contamination have caused severe restrictions in the use of this group.
4. *organophosphates*—malathion and diazinon, have generally replaced the chlorinated hydrocarbons because they control resistant insects, are biodegradable, and do not contaminate the environment.

TABLE 5:2

CLASSIFICATION OF INSECTICIDES ACCORDING TO USE

Adulticides	Larvicides	Ovicides
Space sprays	Solutions	Solutions
Aerosols	Emulsions	Emulsions
Fogs	Suspensions	Fumigants
Mists	Dusts	
Residual sprays	Fumigants	
Fumigants		
Dusts		
Fly cords		
Baits		
Sorptive dusts		
Insecticidal resins		

5. *carbamates*—carbaryl and propoxur, are a relatively new class of contact insecticides that may supplement the organophosphates.
6. *fumigants*—including well-known materials such as naphthalene and paradichlorobenzene (moth crystals) used by the general public, and other very toxic materials, such as methyl bromide or hydrogen cyanide, which are so dangerous that they should be used only by specially trained personnel.

This list gives some idea of the types of chemicals used to kill insects. It does not include the vast numbers of other chemicals used as fungicides and nematocides. Table 5:3 gives a list of the oral and dermal toxicity of selected insecticides.

Toxicity Testing

It is obvious that if we wish to determine the toxic effects of pesticides or any other chemical, we should have a standard method of doing it. It is common practice to do such tests on animals—guinea pigs, rabbits, dogs, or monkeys. The animals

TABLE 5:3

ORAL AND DERMAL TOXICITY OF SELECTED
PUBLIC HEALTH INSECTICIDES VS.
RECOMMENDED STRENGTH OF FINISHED SPRAYS

Insecticide	Acute Oral Toxicity to Female Rats LD_{50} (Mg/kg)*	Acute Dermal Toxicity to Female Rats LD_{50} (Mg/kg)*	Recommended Finished Indoor Spray Concentration (%)
HIGHLY TOXIC INSECTICIDES—Acute oral toxicity to rats—1–50 mg/kg			
ethyl parathion	3.6	6.8	Not used indoors
dioxathion (Delnax)	23	63	0.5
Methyl parathion	24	67	Not used indoors
dieldrin	46	60	0.5
MODERATELY TOXIC INSECTICIDES—Acute oral toxicity to rats—50–500 mg/kg			
dichlorvos (DDVP, Vapona)	56	75	0.6
toxaphene	80	780	
chlorpyrifos (Dursban)	82	202	0.5
propoxur (Baygon)	86	>2400	1.0
lindane	91	900	0.5
Paris green	100	2400	5% outdoor larvicide
DDT	118	2510	5.0
chlordecone (Kepone)	125	2000	0.125 bait
fenthion (Baytex, Entex)	245	330	2.0
dimethoate (Cygon)	245	610	0.5
heptachlor	162	250	
diazinon	285	455	0.5

TABLE 5:3 (continued)

ORAL AND DERMAL TOXICITY OF SELECTED PUBLIC HEALTH INSECTICIDES VS. RECOMMENDED STRENGTH OF FINISHED SPRAYS

Insecticide	Acute Oral Toxicity to Female Rats LD_{50} (Mg/kg)*	Acute Dermal Toxicity to Female Rats LD_{50} (Mg/kg)*	Recommended Finished Indoor Spray Concentration (%)
naled (dibrom)	250+	800+	0.5
chlordane	430	690	2.0–3.0
LOW-ORDER TOXICITY INSECTICIDES—Acute oral toxicity to rats—500–5000 mg/kg			
carbaryl (Sevin)	500	>4000	
trichlorfon (Dipterex)	560	2000	
malathion	1000	>4444	5.0
rabon (Gardona)	1125	>4000	
ronnel (Korlan)	2630	5000	1.0
Mirex	>3000	>2000	
INSECTICIDES COMPARTIVELY FREE FROM DANGER—Acute oral toxicity to rats—5000+ mg/kg			
methoxychlor	6000	>6000	5.0
Temephos (Abate)	13,000	>4000	as outdoor larvicide

*Based on Hayes (28) and Gaines (21), and CDC (10)
+ Data for male rats.
Source: Center for Disease Control: Insecticides for the control of Insects of Public Health Importance. U.S. Department of Health, Education and Welfare. Atlanta, Georgia.

most commonly used are rats and mice. The effects of pesticides on all animals are not the same, and we should therefore try to find those animals that are most like humans—not an easy task.

The whole business of toxicology is complicated, and there are several different types of toxicity test. In the *acute oral* type, the drug is administered in a particular strength as milligrams per kilogram of body weight. The purpose of this test is to find the dosage that will kill 50 per cent of the population being tested, a dosage designated as the LD_{50} figure.

In *subacute oral* toxicity tests, which are of short duration—from three to six months—the object is to find the maximum daily dose that can be consumed by the animal without any demonstrable effect. Then we also try to determine the nature of the effects of the toxicant when administered above the "no effect" level. These subacute tests are particularly important because they include a long period of the animal's life. Observations include daily checking of behavior, general appearance of the animal, assessments of food and water consumption and growth. Blood and urine analyses are made, and other tests may be done as they appear to be necessary. When the test is concluded after 12 or 24 weeks, the animals are killed and the organs examined microscopically. If any abnormalities are found, further studies are undertaken. Some of the best animal pathology we have seen has been carried out in a large commercial laboratory attached to a company that manufactures pesticides.

Chronic oral toxicity tests are carried out on the animals not only over their entire lifetime, but sometimes for several generations. This type of testing is particularly important in connection with the production of cancer and of fetal deformities. In addition to oral testing, there are numerous other tests, including those on the skin or by inhalation.

In research on the effect of pesticides on humans, DDT, with a number of other persistent organochloride insecticides, has been the substance most studied. DDT is not very poisonous to mammals; it has been used directly on humans for louse control. Over the years many thousands of people in malaria eradication programs and in occupational exposure have been exposed to this insecticide without fatality. It would appear that the LD_{50} dosage for a rat is about 200 mg per kg of body weight. A 70 kg person would have to consume about 14 kg of DDT for a lethal dose. Perhaps the saving feature of DDT is that it is not readily damaging to the skin. The skin toxicity in the rat is about 2000 mg per kg.

An entirely more disturbing situation exists with many of the organophosphorus insecticides, such as parathion, that have a high toxicity in mammals, whether the exposure is by mouth or on the skin. Thus it was not surprising that farmers, sprayers, and people who mix insecticides, who had been accustomed to the relatively safe use of DDT, became very ill when they failed to take the safety precautions necessary in handling these more toxic compounds. Organophosphorus poisoning occurs with some frequency, and death from parathion and methyl parathion, as well as related insecticides, may result from small dosages. It has been estimated that in the United States there are at least 100,000 poisonings and 150 deaths from pesticides per year.

Organophosphorus insecticides produce headache, weakness, and fatigue, followed by dizziness and contraction of the pupils. The victim may have trouble focusing. Abdominal cramps set in, accompanied by vomiting and diarrhea, difficulty in breathing, sweating, and excessive salivation, sometimes followed by convulsions, coma, and death.

The first compounds in this group were developed for chemical warfare and are extremely dangerous. Many of the newer compounds, however, have low toxicity to man, domestic animals, and wildlife. These newer materials include malathion, Abate, Ronnel, and others. These insecticides have great value because of their low human toxicity, effectiveness in controlling many species of insects, and biodegradability. They are relatively quickly destroyed and disappear as poisons.

Toxicity of Common Household Chemicals vs. Pesticides

As we have already pointed out, the LD_{50} dose is a dosage at which half of the experimental animals die. If we were to give a specific dose of a chemical to 10 people, and if five of them died, then that dosage is LD_{50}. LD_{50} could also be interpreted as that dose at which a person or animal would have a 50 per cent chance of dying.

Table 5:4 indicates that the LD_{50} in a 154-pound (70 kg)

TABLE 5:4

ESTIMATED LD_{50} DOSE FOR HUMANS, BASED ON RAT EXPERIMENTS, OF COMMON HOUSEHOLD PRODUCTS

POUNDS OF CHEMICALS PER 154 POUND HUMAN

Substance	Amount in pounds
Cleaner, window	4.0
Cloves, ground	6.5
Floorwax, paste	5.0
Horseradish, grated, prepared	6.5
Polish, furniture, liquid	5.0
Sugar, granulated	4.2
Vanilla, extract	4.0
Whiskey (86 proof blended)	5.0
Alcohol, rubbing (Isopropyl alcohol)	1.1
Bleach, liquid (5.25% Sodium hypochlorite)	0.7
Cleanser, all purpose liquid	2.9
Cleanser, powdered	2.0
Cream of tartar	2.3
Detergent, all purpose, granulated	0.9
Gasoline	2.9
Nail polish, liquid	2.9
House paint, white	1.7
Soap, toilet, bath	1.5
Aspirin, acetylacetic acid	0.3
Baking soda (Sodium bicarbonate)	0.5
Table salt	0.7

Source: Hodge, H.C. and Downs, W.L. (1961) Toxicology and Applied Pharmacology 3:689–695

person for ground cloves is 6.5 pounds, the same as for horseradish. To put the toxicity of pesticides into perspective, the LD_{50} dose for sodium chloride—table salt—is 0.7 pounds. The LD_{50} for a herbicide called Tordon 22-K is 1.5 pounds. In other words, this herbicide is less lethal than table salt, because we need half as much table salt at the LD_{50} rate as against 1.5 pounds of the undiluted Tordon 22-K.

Polychlorinated Biphenyls and Polybrominated Biphenyls

The polychlorinated biphenyls or PCBs are synthetic compounds that have been used for industrial purposes for the past 45 years. Because they do not conduct electricity and can withstand high temperatures for long periods, they have been used extensively in the chemical industry and in the electrical industry and in cooling systems. Because they slow degradation, they have also been used as sealants for wood and cement surfaces; they are also used in hydraulic fluids, cutting oils, and in insecticides. Since 1966 scientists throughout the world have been discovering PCBs in a variety of locations where they should not be. The gravity of the threat to human health came to public attention in 1968, when over 1000 Japanese became ill after being exposed to rice oil contaminated with PCBs. In this incident a PCB mixture had been used as a coolant for the oil; holes had developed in the cooling system, and the PCBs were discharged into the rice oil. People who consumed it were exposed to a daily average of about 2 g of the mixture, which is a large dose. They subsequently developed chloracne—a skin condition—headache, nausea and vomiting, peripheral numbness, menstrual irregularity, gastrointestinal disturbance, and many other non-specific signs and symptoms.

We know from animal studies that PCBs can cross the placental barrier and that they are excreted in mother's milk. From these large doses some pregnant women experienced early abortions, and others gave birth to hyperpigmented, hyperkeratotic babies; fortunately, the skin discoloration disappeared as the infants grew older and the effects of the toxicant wore off. Many humans have detectable levels of PCBs in their tissues and continue to accumulate minute amounts. We do not know what the harmful effects may be from long-term, low-level exposure to these compounds, which occur throughout the world.

Much of the polychlorinated biphenyls have been manufactured in the United States, Germany, Italy, Japan, U.S.S.R.,

France, and the United Kingdom. Since 1972, they are no longer made in Japan, and in other countries, such as the United Kingdom and the Federal Republic of Germany, their use has been considerably restricted. They are now being used in closed systems, in dielectric heat transfer, and in hydraulic fluids. Regulations have also been made to restrict the exposure of workers to PCB compounds.

Most people are exposed to PCBs in their food. In a recent study in the United States, it was estimated that the PCB content of a teenage boy's diet was 15 mcg per day in 1971 and 8.7 in 1975. (If this trend is applicable to all of North America, a positive change is taking place.) PCBs are, of course, found in all animal flesh and fish. From a study in two California cities, it was found that the mean PCB level in human milk was 0.06 mcg/ml of whole milk. Infants in these cities ingested about 9 mcg/kg/day of PCBs. In Ontario mean PCB levels in human milk were approximately one mcg/g of fat. Mean levels in human milk in the Federal Republic of Germany were 3.5 mcg/g of the fat portion or 0.1 mcg/ml of whole milk.

In the United States tolerance levels have been established in food. In milk and dairy products it was recently reduced from 2.5 to 1.5 mcg/g; in poultry fat, to 3 mcg/g; in eggs, 0.3 mcg/g; in fish and shellfish, 2 mcg/g. In infant and junior foods the permissible level was laid down as 0.2 mcg/g.

The polybrominated biphenyls (PBBs) are another group of poisonous chemicals that includes three commercial products synthesized in the United States in 1969. The principal PBB product that went into large-scale production in the U.S. was hexabromobiphenyl. Commercial production of an undisclosed amount of hexabromobiphenyl was at first reported by one U.S. company in 1970. It was used as a fire retardant in certain commercial products. In July 1973, in Michigan, cattle feed was accidentally contaminated with about 1000 kg of hexabromobiphenyl and was used by farmers between July 1973 and May 1974. Sickness was first reported in the dairy herd in September 1973, and PBBs were subsequently identified as the toxic factor. In cattle this substance produced loss of appetite, decreased milk production, lameness, hematomas, abscesses, abnormal hoof clefts, alopecia (loss of hair), and skin thickening. Autopsy revealed liver and kidney degeneration, as well as glandular hyperplasia of the major intrahepatic bile ducts of the liver.

Epidemiologic data suggest evidence of a relationship between chronic exposure to polychlorinated biphenyls and the development of malignant melanoma in a small number of cases. Certainly the substance is teratogenic and toxic in rats and mice. It is no longer manufactured in the United States; one company in Germany produces it.

Teratogenicity and Carcinogenicity of Pesticides in Humans

The International Agency for Research in Cancer held a conference in Lyons, France, in 1977–1978 on the evaluation of carcinogenic risk of chemicals to humans. At this meeting were experts from different parts of the world who had been studying or who were interested in this important matter.

Carcinogenesis is the induction of cancer or malignant growth. When we talk about chemical carcinogenesis we mean the induction by chemicals of neoplasms—cancers—that are not usually observed elsewhere; the *earlier* induction by chemicals of neoplasms than is usually observed; and the induction by chemicals of *more* neoplasms than one usually finds. The assessment of carcinogenicity in animals is frequently complicated by recognized differences among animals—the species, strain, sex, age; routes of administration; dose and duration of exposure. We assume that if a chemical induces cancer in a large number of different species of animals, it will also induce cancer in humans, although this is an assumption, not absolute proof.

There are several different ways to study carcinogenicity or production of cancer in humans:

1. considering individual cancer patients or case reports, including the history of exposure to the alleged carcinogenic agent;
2. descriptive epidemiological studies, in which the inci-

dence of cancer in the human populations is found to vary in time and space with exposure to the agent;

3. special analytical epidemiological case-control studies, in which individual exposure to the agent is found to be associated with an increased risk of cancer.

A single epidemiological study may or may not be strongly indicative of carcinogenicity. The most convincing evidence comes from many independent studies done under different circumstances and which result in positive findings. It should be noted that at the present time there is not one single test that identifies all potential carcinogens. There are some tests that are suggestive, and then further work must be done in more detail to determine whether the substance is carcinogenic.

It is often stated that pesticides cause cancer. We do know that a pesticide such as DDT, when given to mice at high dosages, produces tumors, particularly in the liver. The pesticide dieldrin has, in certain instances, produced liver tumors in mice, but it did not produce tumors in rats, chickens, pigeons, monkeys, or dogs. If pesticides cause tumors in humans, particularly liver tumors, we would know it. In fact, primary cancer of the liver is uncommon in Canada and the United States. It is common in Africa, but large-scale use of pesticides has been fairly recent there. We suggest, therefore, that pesticides in general have not caused an increase in the expected types of cancer based on animal experiments.

There is some difference of opinion as to what constitutes a malignant tumor. It would appear that, if the tumor regresses when the toxic agent is withdrawn, then the toxicant is not a carcinogen. The whole question of whether tumors are benign or malignant is important in determining whether chemicals are toxic or not. The matter has not been settled.

There is also a great deal of confusion surrounding the possible mutagenic effects of pesticides. The specter of infant deformity is not to be taken lightly. Many years ago thalidomide was the first drug that was shown very clearly to produce abnormalities in infants. Minimata Disease caused by mercury poisoning produced malformed children from affected parents, and deformed babies have been reported to be associated with the excessive use of defoliants in Vietnam. Good epidemiological evidence from Vietnam has not been obtained because the people of Vietnam have been so dislocated and dispossessed that studies have not been possible.

During recent years there has been a great deal of interest in the herbicide 2,4,5,-T, which is of major importance for weed control in agriculture. Fifty-six scientists who participated in an American Farm Bureau Federation Conference on 2,4,5,-T held in June 1979 concluded that this substance is neither a carcinogen nor a mutagen in animal test systems studied to date. In the past 2,4,5,-T has been contaminated by dioxins, a family of 75 compounds, of which the most thoroughly researched is TCDD (2,3,7,8-Tetrachlorodibenzo-p-toxin). TCDD is teratogenic in 0.1 parts per million, producing cleft palate in mice or killing embryos in a number of experimental species—mouse, rat, hamster, sheep, monkey, and rabbit. In the dosage found there is no evidence that dioxin causes abortions in humans. Controversial epidemiological data came from Alsea, Oregon, and from Seveso in Italy—it would appear that both studies were flawed. There is no evidence that in Oregon there was an increase in abortions in the communities that had been sprayed with 2,4,5,-T, presumably contaminated with TCDD. Evidence from Seveso showed that good epidemiological studies had not been carried out.

We are not suggesting that dioxins are health-promoting chemicals. They are extremely poisonous ones. But in the doses to which pregnant women have been exposed it has not been shown to produce abortions or deformed children.

There is still no evidence that any of the widely used pesticides are carcinogenic, teratogenic, or mutagenic in humans. Some of them have produced pathological effects in laboratory animals, but the dosages were very large. We do not know how to relate these dosages in animals to humans. For example, it is extremely difficult to determine at which point pesticides in mother's milk are harmful to infants. We know that in the past, particularly before DDT was banned, mother's milk had levels as high as 150 parts per million in the early period of infancy. We do not know whether this is harmful or not.

What can be done in this connection is to carry out many detailed, long-term epidemiological studies on humans to see whether strange diseases arise and to see whether we can relate these to toxicants, either from pesticides or other sources. This in itself is an extremely difficult proposition.

The Love Canal

There is every reason that the public in the United States and Canada should be disturbed about what appears to be happening in the Love Canal area in Niagara Falls, New York. We know that at least 21,000 tons of various chemicals were dumped in the Love Canal, and we know that many of these chemicals are toxic. There is no doubt that there have been physical effects on these people. Statements have been made that there have been high rates of miscarriages, stillbirths, and birth defects. Claims have also been made that there have been high rates of cancer, respiratory system disease, and urinary system disease. In this setting, as in others where there may be concentrations of lethal chemicals, the need for sound epidemiological studies is clear and clamant. There can be no proof of the effects of chemicals unless careful, well-designed studies are done with adequate control groups. We know that many of the people living near the Love Canal are ill. It remains for epidemiologists and other medical scientists to find out precisely why, so that similar situations will no longer arise.

Governments in both the United States and Canada have not yet faced the fact that many chemical contaminants exist and chemical contaminants are not being effectively neutralized before being dumped.

6.

Food Poisoning and Parasites

Until comparatively recently, food poisoning from bacterial infection was extremely common. Refrigeration was inadequate or non-existent; there was no sanitary control of slaughterhouses. Meat was contaminated with organisms like *Salmonellae,* and full of parasites, such as tapeworm and trichinosis. As in many Third World countries today, it was not uncommon for people to contract anthrax from eating the meat of animals that had died of this serious disease. Intestinal anthrax arises from the eating of contaminated undercooked meat; the disease itself spreads among herbivorous animals through contaminated soil and feed, and among omnivorous and carnivorous animals from contaminated meat, barn meal, or other feeds. In fact, the role of animal feeds in spreading food infections is extremely important.

Before pasteurization, milk carried a wide variety of bacterial infections, including bovine tuberculosis, diphtheria, Malta fever or brucellosis, and many other infectious diseases. It was not uncommon for cheese to be infected with typhoid bacilli. The fact is that, until recently in human history, food was dangerous. That it is safe now is due to constant vigilance on the part of scientists, conscientious civil servants in many departments of government, as well as local health inspectors. People aren't aware of the tremendous effort that is continually made to keep our food as good as it is. It's still a long way from perfect, however, and the matter of food purity requires continuous and careful attention.

Every year in the United States there are at least 10 million cases of food poisoning, the majority of bacterial origin. Not all of them are reported. In many cases the symptoms, usually diarrhea and nausea, are diagnosed as gastric 'flu; people don't often realize that the infection has come from the food they have eaten.

Dr. Joan Taylor, a world authority on *Salmonella* infections, working at the Central Public Health Laboratory in London, England, has pointed out that there are many similarities in the way of life of human beings and their domestic animals. One of the major changes that has influenced humans has been a dramatic increase in population. In Britain, for example, the population has grown in the last 30 years from 50 million to 56 million. England is now an extremely densely populated country. The same population trend is universal and is especially evident in the Third World. The herding of people in relatively small urban areas has resulted in many meals being prepared in communal settings, such as hotels, schools, restaurants, and canteens. The food is mass-produced on farms, mass-prepared in factories, and then distributed. All over the world protein foods, particularly beef, lamb, pork, poultry, milk, and eggs, are produced in crowded circumstances. In addition, many antibiotics have been given to the animals and subsequently turned up in the foods, with the result that many bacteria have evolved that are resistant to the antibiotics. This is particularly true of the organism *Salmonella*.

Diarrhea

There are many causes of diarrhea, but in most instances the reason is infection by bacteria—*Salmonella, Shigella,* and certain types of *Escherichia coli*. We also know that certain viruses cause diarrhea, but the clinical diseases usually are mild and of short duration. Infections with *Salmonella* and *Shigella* affect all age groups and, although they cause few deaths, these infections are widespread and are a major cause of absenteeism among adults and acute illness in children. Gastroenteritis and deaths from gastroenteritis are common in children under two years of age when these children are crowded together or if they are in large families in the lower socio-economic level. It is now also generally recognized that the incidence of enteritis is much lower in breast-fed infants than in those bottle-fed, even in western countries. This effect is, of course, much more pronounced in the Third World, where artificial formulae for infants are often contaminated by the use of infected water.

Some Cases of Food Poisoning

One of the classic papers on food poisoning is one written by Professor G. N. Dack and his colleagues from the Department of Hygiene and Bacteriology of the University of Chicago. The incriminated food was a three-layer sponge cake with a thick cream filling, ornately iced and decorated with chopped pistachio nuts and maraschino cherries. The cream filling was boiled, one part flavored with vanilla and the other with chocolate. The cake itself was made of flour, whole eggs, sugar, and lemon juice and baked at 300°F for 25 minutes. The eggs were supplied to the bakery in large cans by a commercial egg-cracking company, from 50 to 100 cakes being made from a single can of eggs. These eggs were not refrigerated at the bakery prior to their use.

Two of these cakes were given on the afternoon of December 24 as Christmas presents to the households of two Chicago physicians. The recipients did not keep them in the refrigerator. One cake was served on December 26 at 4:30 p.m. with coffee to three women, including the physician's wife; at about 5:30 for supper to three children, two of them six and one seven years of age; at about 6:00 for supper to the physician, with a second serving to his wife; at 8:00 to a 15-year-old nursemaid who had fed the three children. The other cake was also served on December 26 as part of dinner for three adults.

All 11 people who ate the cake became ill. No one ate the cake without becoming ill. As the victims were from four different families, other foods could easily be eliminated as the cause of illness. Nine of the 11 victims were extremely ill, with vomiting, mild cramps, and severe diarrhea developing from one and a half to four hours after eating. Four of the adults had delayed symptoms of diarrhea, developing 12 and 48 hours after the cake was eaten. Eight people who ate the first cake were quickly ill. The children were prostrated and extremely pale. Two had vomited until the vomit returned clear, and the third boy was just beginning to vomit when the physician saw him. His stomach was aspirated. One of the six-year-old girls passed bloody stools and the other vomited blood. The acute illness lasted about 12 hours.

All the components of the cake were innocuous when fed to monkeys, rabbits, and mice, but when fed to human volunteers the substance of the cake itself proved to contain the toxic factor, a yellow hemolytic *Staphylococcus*. This is a typical instance of staphylococcal food poisoning; it is not the bacterium itself that is poisonous, but an enterotoxin that is produced while the bacterium grows. Several of these enterotoxins are stable even at boiling temperature.

An uncommon type of food poisoning took place in 1974— trichinellosis, acquired at sea. This condition is caused by the migration through the body of the larvae of a parasitic worm called *Trichinella spiralis;* the larvae become encysted in the muscles after the eating of raw or badly cooked pork. The clinical disease in humans is variable. It is usually indicated by a slight fever, but it can be a serious fatal disease. The sudden appearance of a swelling of the upper eyelids is a common and characteristic sign, noted somewhere about the 10th or 11th day after infection. There may be bleeding into the eye, including bleeding into the retina, pain in the eye, and there may also be diarrhea. There is muscle soreness and pain, profuse sweating, weakness, and prostration. There may also be neurological symptoms and heart failure. The distribution of this condition is worldwide. Infected pigs are the commonest source, but the worm may also be found in the meat of wild animals such as wolves and bears, and in dogs, rats, and cats as well.

In October of 1974 in Berkeley, California, a physician

diagnosed trichinosis in a 52-year-old woman, who reported that her husband and a friend who lived elsewhere in California had a similar illness. All had recently returned from a pleasure cruise to Alaska. The ship, with 840 passengers and 450 crew members, had left San Francisco on August 24 and stopped at ports in Canada and Alaska, returning on September 7. This episode was reported to the California State Department of Health, who in turn informed the Center for Disease Control in Atlanta. It was discovered that the hamburger meat served on the cruise had been contaminated with pork, which had obviously been infected.

In 1978, writing in the *New England Journal of Medicine,* Dr. Robert E. Black and colleagues described a fascinating outbreak of food poisoning due to contaminated milk. The first sign of a problem was an alarming increase in appendectomies in a community near Holland Patent, New York. A number of children had shown symptoms of appendicitis, 36 of them were placed in hospital, and 16 had appendectomies. An epidemic of appendectomies is unusual, to say the least. Nevertheless, all the children had been examined individually; they all had abdominal pain and fever, and the diagnosis of appendicitis was made. Those who underwent appendectomies were found to have inflamed and septic appendices.

It was subsequently found, after an excellent epidemiological study, that the illness was associated with the drinking of chocolate milk purchased in a school cafeteria. This milk was contaminated with an organism called *Yersinia enterocolitica,* a less well-known cause of food poisoning. We quote this example to show that food poisoning may result in symptoms that are not always associated with this problem.

On Friday, September 16, 1977, 15 cases of food poisoning were reported to the San Francisco Department of Public Health. All of the people affected had eaten raw tuna and had become ill 15 to 45 minutes later. In nearly all cases typical symptoms of facial flushing and headache were reported, but there were also reports of rash, swollen tongue, abdominal cramps, nausea, diarrhea, rapid heartbeat, and dizziness. One victim gave a particularly interesting account of his illness. He reported that he had dined at a Japanese restaurant on September 13. Forty-five minutes after eating he felt dizziness, abdominal discomfort, "tightness" in his face, itchy eyes, and a dry, swollen tongue. The abdominal discomfort grew steadily worse, followed by violent illness and an enormous amount of diarrhea, which began at midnight, two and a half hours after dinner, and continued for two and a half hours. The abdominal pain persisted through the night and flatulence and weakness were present in the morning. During the next few days he had further bouts of intermittent diarrhea, weakness, and depression. It was not until a week later that he felt better again.

Investigation showed that the disease was associated with raw tuna that was slightly decomposed. The fish contained relatively high levels of histamine, but since histamine is not active when taken by mouth, presumably the presence of histamine was an indicator that another type of poison had been produced by decomposition in the fish. This type of food poisoning, while rare, indicates that many mysterious illnesses may, in fact, be food poisoning, whether they are bacterial in origin, from viruses, or from the byproducts of decomposition, particularly in fish or meat.

Outside of naturally occurring poisons and chemically contaminated food, which we have already discussed, the major types of food poisoning are:

1. Infection of bacterial origin. A good example is salmonellosis. As with other infections and in contrast with poisons, fever is a commonly reported symptom.
2. Poisons from bacteria. Staphylococci or botulinus toxin poisoning are the prime examples; it is not the bacterium, but the toxin it produces, that causes illness. As with chemical poisons, these toxins do not usually produce fever.
3. Infection from a virus. The prime example is hepatitis A. As a result of its long incubation period, about 30 days, identification of the responsible food vehicle can pose a considerable epidemiologic problem.
4. Infections from parasites. We have already mentioned trichinosis from infected pork; other relatively common parasitic diseases are tapeworms, taeniasis, and other worm parasites.

Bacterial Infection

All people eating the same bacterially contaminated food do not necessarily develop food poisoning. If the dose of organisms or viruses is large enough, they will all become ill, whereas if the dose is small only some of them may. One portion of food may contain more bacteria or viruses than others, and individual people may have greater or lesser degrees of resistance to the organism in question.

Salmonellosis is probably the most common bacterial disease in the world. We don't know how many people are infected yearly, because the episodes are not usually reported. The *Salmonella* group of infections was originally described in 1885. There are now approximately 1700 different types of *Salmonella* known, and additional ones are being continuously identified. *Salmonella* infections in humans may range from symptomless carriers to actual illness from the infection, often the result of ingestion of contaminated foods. In the same group of organisms is *Salmonella typhi,* which causes typhoid fever. This disease has disappeared where water standards are high and water is chlorinated, but we can expect it to become more commonplace again all over the world as concentrations of populations increase.

In *Salmonella* outbreaks the origins of the disease in order of frequency, are poultry, various types of meat, people (i.e., from person to person), eggs, dairy products, some pets, such as pet turtles. In most *Salmonella* infections we never determine the origin—in only about one quarter of them can we trace the source. Refrigeration does not destroy the organism, and it can survive for long periods in water, in soil, and in foods. Pasteurization destroys *Salmonella* in milk, and thorough cooking, especially of turkey or chicken, kills the organism.

Salmonellosis is a serious disease in which the organism grows in the human body and the human gut; the incubation period is therefore relatively long, from six to 72 hours, usually about 12 to 36 hours. In preformed toxin, such as in staphylococcal poisoning, the incubation period is very short, something between one to six hours, usually two to four hours.

Some years ago there were many outbreaks of egg-borne

salmonellosis, both in North America and in other parts of the world. Dr. Ernst Ager of the Washington State Department of Health and his colleagues at the University of Washington, Seattle, reported a large-scale outbreak of salmonellosis originating in commercially baked meringue pies. There were two outbreaks, in very close succession, of gastrointestinal disease among students in the same college, a disease characterized by diarrhea, fever, chills, and abdominal cramps. At that time it was found that, from 15,000 cans of frozen egg products used by the bakers of the pies, 20 per cent of them were contaminated with one or more *Salmonella* serotypes.

Contaminated eggs have been a frequent cause of salmonellosis. During World II spray-dried eggs sent to Great Britain from the United States, Canada, and Argentina were apparently responsible for a great increase in salmonellosis outbreaks. The imported dried eggs contained 22 of 33 identified serotypes that had not previously been found in Britain. It is technically possible to produce egg powder that does not carry *Salmonella*, but it is rather difficult, and during the 1960s the dried eggs in many commercial cake mixes were contaminated. That is why cake mixes no longer contain egg powder; the consumer is directed to add fresh eggs to the mix.

Many animal by-products are contaminated with *Salmonella,* too. And as animal feeds contain bone meal and meat meal that may be contaminated, it is extremely difficult to break the cycle. We know also that organic fertilizers can be similarly contaminated, further complicating the elimination of the chain of *Salmonella* spreading from poultry to humans. Poultry feeds can be rendered *Salmonella*-free if they are pelletized with proper heat treatment. But this process is relatively expensive, and we also cannot guarantee that the handling and storage of feeds will be such that recontamination cannot occur.

As food handling is done on an increasingly large scale, there will be many more cases of salmonellosis in the future if great care is not taken. An example of what can happen was a recent common-source outbreak that touched three states in the U.S. The Colorado Department of Health noted a considerable increase in a type of *Salmonella* called *Salmonella newport.* It was found that infected beef hamburger, which came from a processing plant in Dallas, Texas, had reached markets in Colorado, Florida, and Maryland. As our populations increase and as the complexity of our food handling increases, we shall have to be considerably more careful about bacterial food contamination.

For the consumer, the solution to the *Salmonella* problem is to cook all animal foods very carefully. Danger comes from uncooked or rare meat or chicken or egg products, unpasteurized milk, reheated meat and poultry dishes, and various pork products. Cream cakes and pies have also caused many cases of salmonellosis. In order to be sick from *Salmonella*, we have to ingest large numbers of the organisms. If foods are refrigerated quickly and cooled as thoroughly as possible the *Salmonella*, although it will not be killed, will at least not multiply.

Salmonellosis can also be the consequence of unchlorinated water supplies. In 1965 there was a severe epidemic of *Salmonella typhimurium* diarrhea in Riverside, California, more than 15,000 cases, resulting from an unchlorinated public deep water supply. If we do not take care of our water supply, particularly in times of civil disruption, we may find many more cases of salmonellosis than we would bargain for.

Other Bacteria

Another common bacterial cause of food poisoning is *Clostridum perfringens* of the type A strains. Most of these organisms are found in the soil and also in the gastrointestinal tract of humans and domestic animals. This type of food poisoning is usually associated with inadequately heated or reheated meats, usually meat pies, gravies, stews, or chicken, turkey, or beef. The spores survive normal cooking temperatures, and they multiply during cooling and rewarming. Outbreaks of this type are usually found in restaurants, cafeterias, and schools, resulting from inadequate cooking and refrigeration facilities and large-scale service. Fortunately, heavy bacterial contamination is necessary for disease to result.

Another bacterial culprit is *Vibrio parahaemolyticus*. Illness caused by this organism is characterized by abdominal cramps

and watery diarrhea, with nausea, vomiting, fever, and headache. It is found in raw seafood or seafood cooked too little to
destroy the naturally occurring *Vibrio,* or cooked seafood that
has been cross-contaminated by the handling of raw seafood.
The incubation period is 12 to 24 hours. A somewhat less
common cause of food poisoning is *Bacillus cereus.* Its spores
are heat resistant, and it is found in the soil and in foodstuffs,
but it is not common in North America.

Bacterial Poisons

In most cases this type of poisoning can be distinguished from
that caused by metals or chemicals by the absence of fever.
Staphylococcal enterotoxin food poisoning is widespread and
relatively frequent, in fact one of the commonest types in North
America. It is transmitted by the consumption of many foods—
pastries, salads, sandwiches, meat products. The *Staphylococci* may originate with infected food handlers, or they may
come from infected cows and the resultant contaminated milk
products. They are also sometimes found in ham and bacon.
The interval between eating the food and development of
symptoms is one to six hours.

Botulism is not an infection like *Salmonellosis,* but rather
the result of a poison produced by a bacterium, *Clostridium
botulinum.* This disease is characterized by extreme dryness
of the mouth, weakness, and paralysis of the eye muscles.
There is sometimes sore throat, double vision, vomiting, and
diarrhea, and sometimes constipation. The most worrying
symptoms are neurological ones: Paralysis of the external muscles
of the eye and paralysis of the muscles of the pharynx due to
respiratory failure. About one third of the victims die within
three to seven days.

In North America the disease is usually caused by
contaminated food, mainly from jars or cans that have been
inadequately processed during canning and eaten without
subsequent adequate cooking. The major sources are home-
canned vegetables, fruits, fish, and more rarely meat. In Europe
most cases are due to sausages or smoked or preserved meats

or fish. In Canada a number of cases are due to special foods prepared by native peoples.

The toxin is produced only under anaerobic conditions— i.e., in which there is no oxygen—and especially in low-acid foods. The toxin is destroyed by boiling, but the inactivation of the spores requires higher temperatures. Ordinary refrigeration does not necessarily prevent toxin production. Human botulism is rare, but it is a persistent hazard in some areas; there is an almost endemic occurrence of botulism among Eskimos in Alaska, the Canadian North West Territories, and Labrador. There have recently been outbreaks of fish-borne botulism in the United States, and there have been a few recent cases in which infants have died of botulism. The clinical findings include constipation, weak sucking and crying ability, some damage to the cranial nerves, general weakness, and sudden cessation of breathing—symptoms that are not easily diagnosed.

Viruses

The most common form of virus food poisoning is hepatitis A. It is spread from person to person through the fecal-oral route and by water and is most common in lower socio-economic settings where there is overcrowding. One of the largest urban outbreaks in modern history occurred in 1956 in Delhi, India, where over 25,000 cases were attributed to contaminated water supplies. In North America contaminated food is a common cause of outbreaks. A wide variety of food items, which are usually contaminated by food handlers who are in the incubation period of disease, have been incriminated as vehicles— bakery goods, milk, fish, cold meats, and salads. Raw shellfish have also been responsible, particularly raw clams and oysters harvested from sewage-contaminated water, which has resulted in several outbreaks in the United States and elsewhere. The effects of hepatitis A will no doubt increase as human populations increase and as the environment becomes fouler.

There are many different kinds of viruses that can cause food poisoning, usually milk infections that are diagnosed as gastric 'flu. Their transmission mechanism is unknown; it is probably by the fecal-oral route, with the infected person's hands contaminating food. Sporadic viral gastroenteritis is probably also spread by the fecal-oral route, although its mode of transmission has not been clearly worked out. There is still a great deal of study to be done in the area of virus enteritis.

Parasitic Infections

The commonest parasitic infections, caused by infected meat, are trichinellosis and tapeworm. We have already mentioned infection by the larvae of *Trichinella spiralis,* which affect the muscles of the host if he or she has eaten insufficiently cooked infected meat. And the meat is usually pork, although the disease can be acquired from bear meat. This condition still exists in North America and it is difficult to control. All fresh pork and pork products should be well cooked, so that all parts have a temperature of at least 65.6°C (150°F), or until the meat changes from pink to gray. If hunters must eat bear meat, they should cook it very thoroughly. Low temperatures will also kill the *Trichinae,* but at least 20 days storage at −25°C is required.

Tapeworms are acquired by eating raw or undercooked meat infected with the larval stage (the cysticercus) of *Taenia.* Either pork or beef can carry these larvae, which develop into adult worms in the human intestine. Even non-infected meat can be contaminated by infected food handlers, whose feces harbor tapeworm eggs. These eggs are infective immediately upon leaving the host, and they produce a severe and incurable illness.

Prevention of Food Poisoning

As Dr. Frank L. Bryan has pointed out, in most outbreaks of food-borne disease, foods identified as vehicles are found to have been mishandled during preparation, in food-processing plants, institutional kitchens, even in the home. Examples of

TABLE 6:1

OPERATIONS THAT CONTRIBUTED TO THE OCCURRENCE OF 235 OUTBREAKS OF FOODBORNE DISEASE THAT RESULTED FROM FOODS MISHANDLED IN FOOD SERVICE ESTABLISHMENTS, 1973 THROUGH 1975.

Rank	Operations (factors) that contributed to outbreaks	Number		Per cent	
		Category	Specific factor	Category	Specific factor
	Direct factors affecting growth	210		89	
1	Improper cooling (such as leaving cooked foods at room temperature and storing foods in large pots and other containers in refrigerators)		148		63
3	Improper hot-holding		62		27
	Indirect factors affecting growth	84		36	
2	Lapse of a day or more between preparing and serving (coupled with inadequate storage practices)		68		29
6	Use of leftover foods (coupled with inadequate storage practices)		16		7
	Factors affecting survival	71		30	
5	Inadequate reheating of previously		59		25

TABLE 6:1 (continued)

OPERATIONS THAT CONTRIBUTED TO THE OCCURRENCE OF 235 OUTBREAKS OF FOODBORNE DISEASE THAT RESULTED FROM FOODS MISHANDLED IN FOOD SERVICE ESTABLISHMENTS, 1973 THROUGH 1975.

Rank Operations (factors) that contributed to outbreaks	Number		Per cent	
	Category	Specific factor	Category	Specific factor
cooked foods				
9 Inadequate cooking of raw foods		12		5
Factors affecting contamination	122		52	
4 Infected persons (usually nasal carriers of *Staphylococcus aureus* touching cooked foods)		61		26
7 Improper cleaning of kitchen equipment (such as slicers, grinders, cutting boards, preparing knives, storage pots)		21		9
8 Cross-contamination of pathogenic microorganisms on raw foods of animal origin to foods that are cooked or that require no further heating		15		6

TABLE 6:1 (continued)

OPERATIONS THAT CONTRIBUTED TO THE OCCURRENCE OF 235 OUTBREAKS OF FOODBORNE DISEASE THAT RESULTED FROM FOODS MISHANDLED IN FOOD SERVICE ESTABLISHMENTS, 1973 THROUGH 1975.

Rank Operations (factors) that contributed to outbreaks	Number		Per cent	
	Category	Specific factor	Category	Specific factor
via workers' hands or equipment				
10 Storing low-acid foods in toxic metal containers		9		4
11 Contaminated raw ingredient eaten raw or insufficiently cooked		5		2
12 Intentional additives of poisonous substances in excessive quantities		5		2
13 Additives reaching foods from carelessness, accidents, improper storage, or mistaken as food ingredients		3		1
14 Foods obtained from unsafe sources		2		1
15 Contaminated water		1		≤1

problem areas are infected persons touching cooked foods or equipment that previously touched raw foods of animal origin. In an excellent article recently in the *Journal of Environmental Health*, he outlines the kitchen techniques that are needed to stop the development of food poisoning, summarized in Table 6:1, including improper cooling, improper methods of keeping food hot, elapsed time between preparing and serving food, the use of leftover foods, inadequate reheating of previously cooked foods, inadequate cooking of raw foods. What are often forgotten are the factors that effect contamination. Foremost are infected persons, usually carriers of *Staphylococcus aureus*, touching cooked foods; next comes improper cleaning of kitchen equipment; cross-contamination of organisms on raw foods of animal origin to foods that are cooked or that require no further heating, via work with hands or equipment; storage of low-acid foods in toxic metal containers; and insufficient cooking of contaminated raw meat. A small number of cases are caused by poisonous additives reaching foods by accident or through carelessness, and by foods obtained from unsafe sources, such as unpasteurized milk.

---

*Data about raw foods bringing pathogens into food service establishments are seldom available and are not included in this listing, but they are important sources of contamination.

Source: Bryan, F. L. (1979) Prevention of Foodborne Diseases In Food Service Establishments. Journal of Environmental HealthVol. 41. No. 4, pp. 198–206.

7.

Water in Health and Disease

Water is the main component of the human body, forming about two thirds of our total body weight. While oxygen is the most important part of our environment, water comes a close second. We cannot live without it for more than a few days. Dehydration kills far more quickly than starvation. In Northern Ireland, where people went on hunger strikes, one man survived 53 days of not eating; he did, however, keep up his supply of water and salt. A human being can lose most of his fat and half the protein—that is, 40 per cent of body weight—and still survive. About a 20 per cent loss of body water may cause death, and a loss of only 10 per cent causes severe disorders.

If we exclude fat from the body about 70 per cent of the mass of the fat-free body weight consists of water:
  (a) intracellular water, contained within the cells of the body, about 50 per cent of body weight;
  (b) extracellular water, including water in the blood, lymph, spinal fluid, and secretions—about 5 per cent;
  (c) intracellular water, found between and around the cells—about 15 per cent of body weight.
The distribution of body water is not fixed. It varies under different circumstances, but the total amount remains relatively constant.

Water is the solvent in which all metabolic activities in the body take place. Furthermore, it takes an active part, as a catalyst, in many body processes. It is obviously essential in the processes of digestion, absorption, circulation, and excretion. We all know that it leaves the body through the skin as perspiration, from the lungs in the breath, from the kidneys as urine, and from the intestines as feces. It is very important that the salts and electrolytes in the body exist in correct proportions, and this is directly linked to water balance in the body. In diseases involving severe diarrhea, there is a very rapid loss of fluid through the alimentary tract, resulting in a considerable loss of electrolytes, particularly sodium and potassium. In fact, what kills people with severe diarrhea, such as in cholera, is electrolyte loss. Dehydration can kill small infants very easily. Adults are more resistant, but if there is a great deal of water and electrolyte loss through the gut, death follows. Therefore, the treatment of diarrhea consists of giving water with a little salt or potassium in it by mouth. If this is not possible, electrolytes are provided intravenously, either in the form of glucose and salt solutions or as blood, plasma, or protein mixtures.

Water also plays a role in maintaining body temperature. During warm weather and in fever, sweating keeps the skin moist; as the sweat evaporates, the body is cooled. Water also acts as a method of transport for body substances, such as enzymes or hormones. Waste products manufactured by the body are dissolved in water and excreted by the blood through the kidneys, where the wastes are dissolved in urine. Water in the body acts as a lubricant; saliva, which makes food slippery, contains water. In our joints we have lubricating fluids that contain water as well as other substances; as we get older we start creaking a bit as our bodies contain less water. Water also acts as a building material for the process of growth and repair of the body. There is no part of the body that does not contain water.

The Balance of Water

Healthy people depend on the mechanism of thirst to determine their water intake; the thirst control center is situated in the midbrain. Most adults consume somewhere between 1.5 to 2 ℓ

of fluid daily. In addition, most foods contain some water, and the foods we eat produce water when oxidized. One hundred g of fat, carbohydrate, or protein yield, respectively, 107, 55, and 45g of water. The water in our body produced as a result of oxidation of food per hundred kilocalories is about 10 to 14g or about 300 to 350 ml per day. In the process of water balance, a large amount of the extracellular fluid is transferred into the stomach and the intestines to help the digestive process, as much as 8 l per day. On the other hand, most of this water is then reabsorbed in the end of the large intestine. How the body's water balance works is shown in Table 7:1. Water intake must balance water output, and does in a healthy body. Table 7:2 shows how much water some common foods contain.

In every healthy person, then, there is a balance of water. When people are ill in the hospital, it is important to maintain charts on water balance to see whether they are losing or retaining fluid. The determination of water balance is most accurately carried out by frequent weighing of the individual, combined with a record of fluid intake and urine and bowel output.

It is extremely important to ensure that small children get

TABLE 7:1

WATER BALANCE

WATER INTAKE

Fluids	1250 ml.
Water in food	900 ml.
Water from oxidation of food in the body	350 ml.
Total	2500 ml.

WATER OUTPUT

Urine	1400 ml.
Water in feces	100 ml.
Skin (perspiration)	700 ml.
Lungs (expired air)	300 ml.
Total	2500 ml.

TABLE 7:2

PERCENTAGE OF WATER IN SOME COMMON FOODS

Lettuce (iceberg)	96
Snapbeans, radishes, celery	94
Watermelon	93
Cabbage (raw)	92
Broccoli, carrots, beets, collards	91
Orange	88
Milk	87
Cereals (cooked)	87
Apples	85
Potatoes (boiled)	80
Bananas	76
Eggs	74
Corn	74
Chicken (boiled)	71
Fish (baked)	68
Prunes (cooked)	66
Beef (lean)	60
Cheese	40
Bread	36
Cake (sponge)	32
Butter	16
Nuts	5
Soda crackers, dry cereals	4
Sugar (white)	trace
Oils	0

Source: Nutritive Value of Foods, U.S. Department of Agriculture. Home Garden Bull. No. 72, revised 1964.

enough fluid, particularly in warm weather. Infants on high protein formulas must have a great deal of water. And anyone who lives or works in a hot environment or who is suffering from fever will need to consume more water to maintain the balance.

The average adult needs a daily total of 2500 to 4500 mℓ of water, which is added to a body pool of 30 to 50 ℓ. Many women experience large swings in water balance in relation to the menstrual cycle. The amount of urine secreted by an adult is something between 1000 and 3000 mℓ per day. When outputs fall to 400 or 600, the urine is greatly concentrated. On the other hand, if there is a large protein intake or illness there may be a considerable increase in the urine volume.

Humans and Water

Our need for water is obvious. What may not be so obvious is the enormous problem facing us in filling the world-wide need for fresh water. Until about 1950 we could easily extend the earth's cropland to increase the world supply of food. But since that time, world population has outstripped the availability of land. Today there is less than half a hectare for each of the world's almost five billion people. The earth cannot expand. Most of the good cropland has already been worked. At the same time, while unexploited fertile land is scarce, the lack of fresh water may be the final constraint on the efforts to expand world food output. There is a vast and growing lack of fresh water, not only in Mexico and Afghanistan, but in California and many parts of the southwestern and central United States.

In the Soviet Union the lack of fresh water is limiting the production of feed grains, which are needed for the increase in Russian livestock. In many countries the competition for water is becoming increasingly fierce—between Israel and the Arab countries for the waters of the Jordan, between the Sudan and Egypt for the waters of the Nile. As time goes on, many irrigation options are exhausted.

We know that irrigated forms of agriculture supplied the surplus food and the impetus for social organization in ancient Mesopotamia and Egypt. In China there has been a great increase in the amount of irrigated land, the result of a systematic effort in the massive mobilization of rural labor in off-season times. Both in the Soviet Union and in North America tremendous plans have been laid to divert fresh water into areas where more water is needed. However, these plans will come to a halt, because there are limits to the number of people that the earth can bear, no matter how much we try to modify the laws of nature.

It is interesting that, as diets improve, we need more water to produce our food. For example, if a vegetarian eats 2½ pounds of grain a day (about 1 kg) 300 gallons of water (about 1400 ℓ) are required for its production. On the other hand, if a person consumes 2 pounds of vegetable matter and 1 pound of beef and animal fat a day, 2500 gallons of water are required to produce it. The water cost of a pound of beef, a little less than half a kilogram, including the water to produce the feed as well as that required by the animal, amounts to about 25 times that needed to produce an equal amount of bread.

We are running out of water. There are times when even New York feels drought. As populations grow and as their water becomes more polluted, the problem will be vastly aggravated. The world's major rivers—the Yellow, the Ganges, the Colorado, the Nile—have been exploited almost to their capacity. Irrigation from the Mekong in Vietnam and the Amazon have remained unexploited, but another concern affects the Amazon: tearing down the forests might be far more serious in terms of soil erosion than the usefulness of the water. In many parts of the world, particularly in parts of Africa, Asia, and the United States, the drilling of wells will provide a temporary source of water, but as the ground water declines, many of these areas within measurable time will have no water. In the United States the dramatic increase in the number of wells and amount of irrigation in the western great plains and the southwest have resulted in a drop in the water tables. In some areas close to the sea, seawater has seeped into the wells.

Natural History of Water

Where does water come from? All water comes from water vapor condensed in the form of rain or snow. Some of this returns to the atmosphere by evaporation, while the rest collects upon the surface of the earth or soaks into the ground. We draw our water supplies from three sources: rain or snow water; surface water, including lakes, streams, and rivers; and ground water, including springs and wells. This is a simple and arbitrary classification; there is no sharp distinction between rain, surface, and ground water. Rainwater soon becomes surface water, and surface water may quickly pass into the ground.

Rainwater in itself is not commonly used in industrialized areas of the world, as it is difficult to collect it in such a way as to render it free from pollution and fit for drinking. Furthermore, at present rainwater in many parts of the world is contaminated, particularly with sulfuric acid. The sulfuric acid comes from the sulfur dioxide produced by the burning of coal and some types of oil containing sulfur. At any rate in most localities it is not feasible to collect and store enough rainwater to support the large demand of a modern community. In Bermuda and some of the islands of the Caribbean, rainwater is collected, but there are increasing difficulties as their populations grow. In the collection of rainwater care must be taken that the collecting surface is clean and that the first flow, which contains most of the bacterial and other impurities, is separated. The location and construction of the storage system are very important. Concrete storage systems are usually placed underground, while wooden ones are placed above ground. Because rainwater attacks iron, lead, zinc, and other metals, the material used for plumbing must be carefully scrutinized. Naturally, lead systems and surface pipes should not be employed for rainwater that will be used for drinking purposes. Sand filters are often used to filter the rainwater, but filters without expert care are of dubious value.

Surface water from an inhabited watershed is never safe to drink because it has been contaminated by human and animal feces. Our water supplies in North America and Europe are obtained from lakes and dammed rivers and undergo extensive filtering, purification, and disinfection. However, water treatment only removes solid impurities and bacteria. It cannot remove many chemicals. As industrialization proceeds, it will be the chemicals in the water that will cause problems. At present there are so many new chemicals being produced that we do not know what they can do and will do as a health hazard.

How Water is Purified

In nature, water is purified by various methods, the chief of which is evaporation, followed by condensation, which makes rainwater the purest of natural water. If there were few people on earth, storage in lakes and ponds would clarify rainwater and in time eliminate impurities, and the physical, chemical, and biological action of the soil upon water as it filters through the earth is one of nature's greatest purifying agents. But these natural processes can only take place where human populations are small. They cannot function where there is vast overcrowding, which now exists in most parts of the world.

So humans must intervene in water purification, and many processes are used. The first is to aerate the water, which helps to diminish flavors or odors. Then the water is coagulated by treatment with various chemicals, such as aluminum sulfate, so that organisms and metals like iron and manganese form flocks and can be screened out. The next stage is to let the water stand to bring about the process of sedimentation; the heavier elements in the water, including bacteria, sink to the bottom. The next part of the process is filtration; the water may be filtered through charcoal or various types of sand. Then it is softened by the removal of the salts that produce hard water. Otherwise these salts would form deposits on plumbing, boilers, and kettles; furthermore, soap does not lather easily in hard water, making washing difficult.

At last the water is disinfected, usually by judicious and wise use of chlorine, which kills unwanted organisms and also removes odors and flavors. Sometimes bromine or ozone are used instead. If odors and flavors are not sufficiently removed by chlorination, they can be removed by putting the water through activated carbon.

One of the objectives of water treatment is to stop it from being too corrosive. If water is too acid, it will dissolve metals in pipes, and the metals themselves may be detrimental to health—lead, for example.

Water-Borne Diseases

In developed countries, water does not usually spread disease because it is purified and disinfected. But it is relatively recently in our history that such has been the case. It was not long ago in North America that there were widespread outbreaks of diarrheal diseases, such as typhoid and dysentery, that could be traced to contaminated water supplies. It is not unknown even today for visitors to the Soviet Union to come back with an infection known as *Giardia lamblia,* which almost certainly comes from Russian water supplies. In Third World countries disease from contaminated water is normal; many people walk around with and die from diarrheal diseases.

Tables 7:3, 7:4, and 7:5 outline the diseases borne by water, particularly in those parts of the world where there is not enough money to build water treatment facilities. The bacterial diseases are bacillary dysentery and cholera, and there are many other diarrheal diseases, such as paratyphoid and typhoid, among the most important of the water-borne diseases. Cholera has now spread to many parts of the world. A few years ago it was confined mainly to Asia, but it has now spread to the whole of Africa, from north to south. This disease can be controlled if people have access to a clean water supply, but in many parts of Africa there are none.

Certain viruses may also be spread by water, and there is some question whether our methods of disinfection of these viruses actually kill them. Other diseases are caused by protozoa or worms (helminths), including amoebic dysentery, giardiasis, and a number of others. It has also been felt that certain fungal infections may be spread through water supplies. Water-washed diseases may come either from contact with water, or from a lack of water, as in trachoma, a serious eye disease. There are other eye infections among the water-washed diseases, and it is possible that leprosy may be spread in this way.

One of the most serious diseases induced by the environment in vast numbers of people is schistosomiasis. This is a tropical disease in which worms infect the human body after it is exposed to water in which the organisms swim. The disease is unknown in industrial societies, but it is now thought to afflict something like 200 million people in Africa, southeast

TABLE 7:3

WATERBORNE DISEASES THAT MAY BE OF FECAL ORIGIN

1. Bacterial Diseases

    Bacillary dysentery (*Shigella* spp.)
    Cholera *(Vibrio cholerae)*
    Diarrhoeal disease and gastroenteritis (etiology
        unknown, possibly *Yersinia enterocolytica,*
        enteropathogenic, *E. coli, Vibrio parahaemolyticus* or
        any of several other enterobacterial species.
    Leptospirosis (*Leptospira* spp.)
    Paratyphoid (*Salmonella* spp.)
    Typhoid (*Salmonella* typhi)
    Tularemia *(Francisella tularensis)*

2. Viruses

    Enteroviruses (Coxsackie A & B, Polio, Echo, Other
        Enteroviruses)
    Hepatitis A
    Adenoviruses
    Reoviruses and Rotaviruses
    Viruses that may cause gastroenteritis and diarrhoeal
        disease of unknown etiology (Norwalk-type viruses)

3. Protozoan and Helminth Diseases

    Amoebic dysentery *(Entamoeba histolytica)*
    Ascariasis *(Ascaris lumbricoides)*
    Balantidiasis *(Balantidium coli)*
    Enterobiasis *(Enterobius vermicularis)*
    Giardiasis *(Giardia intestinalis* or *G. lamblia)*
    Trichuriasis *(Trichuris trichiura)*

4. Fungal Infections
    Candida species and other yeasts

Asia, mainland China, the Caribbean, and the northeastern
coast of South America. Estimates have been made that, in
these areas, seven out of nine rural habitants suffer this disease.
It is spreading rapidly, particularly in Africa, where irrigation
schemes have been expanded while good sanitation is non-
existent.

TABLE 7:4

WATER-WASHED DISEASES

1. Bacterial Diseases

    Eye infections (*Bacillus subtilis* and *Vibrio
        parahaemoliticus*)
    Leprosy *(Mycobacterium leprae)*
    Opportunistic infections (i.e., *Pseudomonas* spp. and
        Staphylococcus spp.)
    Yaws *(Treponema pertenue)*

2. Viruses

    Adenoviruses
    Rhinoviruses
    Some Enteroviruses

3. Miscellaneous Microorganisms

    Conjunctivitis (*Chlamydiae* and *Leptospira*)
    Mycotic infections
    Opportunistic infections *(Candida albicans)*
    Trachoma (Chlamydiae)
    Typhus *(Rickettsia)*

The disease cycle is this: Eggs of the worm are shed
through human urine and feces and get into the water supplies.
Part of their life cycle is spent within certain snails, then the
adult worm is released to swim in the water supply again and
reinfect human beings.

Political leaders in poor tropical countries keep on building new irrigation schemes without consideration for the health
risks of schistosomiasis. It is good to increase food production,
but not at the cost of the health of large sections of the population.

Water Pollution

At the time of writing it would appear that in the United States
there is going to be a weakening of federal regulations concerning air and water pollution. We hope this will not happen. We

TABLE 7:5

POTENTIALLY WATER-BORNE DISEASES
WORLDWIDE

Roundworms
  Ascaris lumbricoides
Amoebic dysentery
  Entamoeba histolytica
Primary amebic
Meningoencephalitis—
  Naegleria and
  Acanthamoeba
Hepatic capillariasis
  Capillaria hepatica
Cholera
  Vibrio cholerae
Diarrhea
Enteropathogenic
  Escherichia coli
Dracontiasis
  Dracunculus medinensis
Giardiasis
  Giardia lamblia
Viral hepatitis
  Hepatitis A

Hydatiodosis
  Echinococcus
Leptospirosis
  Leptospira
Melioidosis
  Pseudomonas pseudomallei
Paratyphoid fever
  Salmonella paratyphic A
  Salmonella schottmuelleri
Other Salmonella infections
Schistosomiasis
  Schistosoma mansoni
  S. *haematobium*
  S. *japonicum*
Typhoid fever
  Salmonella typhi
Shigellosis
  Shigella dysenteriae
  Sh. *flexneri*
  Sh. *boydii*
  Sh. *sonnei*

know that there is still a great deal of raw sewage coming into the Great Lakes. Sewage waste treatment facilities to eliminate phosphorus and other harmful pollutants have been delayed in Detroit, Buffalo, Cleveland, Syracuse, Akron, and other places on the U.S. side of the basin. On the Canadian side full sewage treatment has not yet been completed in Thunder Bay, Cornwall, and Sault Ste. Marie. Montreal still floats in a sea of sewage.

If sewage were the only problem we could possibly cope. But the biggest problems are not the results of sewage in water, but the vast amounts of chemicals that have been placed in our water supplies. The Niagara area is a terrible example. The Niagara River itself has been a chemical dumping ground for years, and the Love Canal is well known for its chemically polluted ground water. During the 1960s phosphates from sewage and high-phosphate detergents helped to fertilize algae and weeds, promoting the growth that choked harbors and rotted on beaches. Many species of fish died off as they were unable to reproduce in the foul waters.

Since 1945 vast numbers of new chemicals have been developed, and many of them have found their way into the water. Most of the time we do not know exactly what these chemicals will do to people, and we do not know at what concentration in water they become harmful. It costs at least three years and up to three million dollars to do a study of just one organic compound to determine whether or not it will produce disease. If we mix up a number of chemicals, the whole testing procedure becomes incredibly more complicated. Furthermore, we know that very small amounts of certain chemicals do not kill fish, but when these fish are eaten by others, at the final stage, at the top predator, there are high concentrations of poisons, ranging from mercury to PCBs.

As far as we know at the moment people are not being harmed by chemicals in the water. But what of the future? It may take 20 years or more before any effects are manifested, and then it will be difficult to determine what produces particular effects. There are in the region of 50 thousand chemicals in commercial production that may be a health risk as many of them are toxic and they accumulate in the environment. In the United States more than 57 million metric tons of chemical wastes are created each year. In the province of Ontario at least 263,000 tons of liquid industrial waste is disposed of each year. And as we know, a lot of this disposal is inefficient, ineffective, and illegal. We often do not even know where the dumps are or where they have been.

As industrialization proceeds, chemical pollution of water increases, whether from asbestos mining, pulp and paper wastes, chemical wastes from chemical companies, phenols and cyanides from steel-processing plants, and many others. Agriculture, as well as industry, damages the water supply through pesticide and fertilizer runoff.

So far more than 300 organic chemicals have been identified in drinking water supplies in North America. These substances come from industry, from cities, from natural decomposition of plant and animal matter, and from the reaction of some chemicals with chlorine in water treatment. Testing for these chemicals requires experienced chemists and expensive and sophisticated instruments. Some of the large water supply laboratories are equipped with atomic absorption spectrophotometers for measuring metals; on the other hand, the gas chromatograph mass spectrophotometers required for measuring synthetic organic chemicals are extremely expensive, and only a few laboratories have enough money to buy these machines and pay for the highly trained people to operate them.

Table 7:6, from the U.S. Environmental Protection Agency, gives the maximum contaminant levels for various chemicals in the water. Some of these levels are approximate, and one hopes that, as time goes by, we will accumulate more scientific evidence on which to base accurate standards.

Nitrates, Fluorides, and Sodium

It is of some interest that a disease called methemoglobinemia has occurred in infants after they have consumed well water containing nitrates in concentrations of greater than 100 mg/ℓ of nitrogen. About 2000 cases of this disease have been reported in North America and Europe. It results from the change in the

TABLE 7:6

NATIONAL INTERIM PRIMARY DRINKING WATER REGULATIONS* (MAXIMUM CONTAMINANT LEVELS—MCL)

Contaminant	MCL
Inorganic chemicals	
Arsenic	0.05 (mg/liter)
Barium	1
Cadmium	0.010
Chromium	0.05
Lead	0.05
Mercury	0.002
Nitrate (as N)	10
Selenium	0.01
Silver	0.05
Fluoride	1.4–2.4

TABLE 7:6 (continued)

NATIONAL INTERIM PRIMARY DRINKING WATER REGULATIONS* (MAXIMUM CONTAMINANT LEVELS—MCL)

Contaminant	MCL
Organic chemicals	
Chlorinated hydrocarbons	
Endrin	0.0002
Lindane	0.004
Methoxychlor	0.1
Toxaphene	0.005
Chlorophenoxyls	
2,4-D	0.1
2,4,5-T, Silvex	0.01
Turbidity	1 unit
Microbiologic contaminants	1 coliform bacterium per 100 ml as the arithmetic mean of all samples per month
Radioactivity	
Combined radium-226 and radium-228	5 pCi/liter
Gross alpha particle activity (including radium-226 but excluding radon and uranium)	5 pCi/liter 15 pCi/liter
Average annual concentration of beta particle and photon radioactivity not to produce annual dose equivalent greater than	4 millirem per year
Tritium	20,000 pCi/liter
Strontium-90	8 pCi/liter

*Environmental Protection Agency, 1976. United States of America.

gastrointestinal tract of nitrates to nitrites, which then change the hemoglobin to methemoglobin, which cannot transport oxygen. The babies turn blue and become very ill or die. Mothers should therefore know about the nitrate content of water if they draw from wells.

We know that fluorine is important in maintaining good teeth, but if water contains too much fluorine, people may suffer from fluorosis, a disease of the bones and teeth.

A further complication that may exist in water is that it may contain too much sodium. We know that too much sodium chloride increases the blood pressure, and that certain heart patients need to restrict their sodium intake. Softening water by ion exchange adds considerable amounts of sodium to water supplies, so that home water softeners may not be an unmixed blessing. From work done by Dr. T. W. Anderson and Dr. L. C. Neri, there appears to be a relationship between water and ischemic heart disease; soft water to some extent seems to predispose to the development of coronary thrombosis.

The Future

In North America there are many contaminated water supplies, particularly those contaminated by noxious chemicals. In the United States there has recently been evidence that ground water supplies have been contaminated by chemicals from chemical dumps. This is a serious problem which so far has not been effectively faced, either in Canada or the United States.

It is possible to clean up water supplies. A classic case is that of the River Thames in England, which is now much cleaner than it has been for the last 100 years. Another river that is much cleaner than it used to be is the Cuyahoga, which winds through industrial Cleveland. As recently as 1970 the oily surface of this river caught fire. Today in the same area people are returning to the banks of the river and the fish are returning to its waters.

Both politicians and manufacturers have been reluctant to clean the water supplies and to clean the air. It will take a great deal of public pressure to make them understand that we are now creating a physical environment that within the next few years will have deleterious effects on our health. So far we do not know what these effects will be. But by the time the effects are measurable, it will cost vast sums of money to clean up the environment. We may never be able to do it.

8.

Drugs in Pregnancy

The following statement is from a standard work in pharmacology by Goodman and Gilman, *The Pharmacological Basis of Therapeutics:*

> Women are thought to be more susceptible than men to the effects of certain drugs, in part because of smaller size. In some instances, this difference is considered sufficient to necessitate reduction in dosage.
>
> During pregnancy, caution is necessary in the administration of drugs that might affect the uterus or fetus. A wise precaution is to avoid the use of all drugs, except those essential to maintain pregnancy and the health of the mother (i.e., iron salts, folic acid).

We know that certain cancer treatment drugs—aminopterin, methotrexate, and others—used during pregnancy may lead to embryonic death or deformity. These drugs would not be commonly used, but they have been. Certain hormonal substances may also produce deformities in children; drugs related to testosterone have been used to prevent abortion, producing variable degrees of masculinity of unborn females. The teratogenic or deformity-producing effects of thalidomide are well known. Discovered in 1961, they include deformities of the limbs, usually of a characteristic pattern, defects of the eyes and ears, and malformations of many organs, including the heart. We know that cortisone and related drugs easily cause malformations in some experimental animals; in humans, there is some evidence that there might be a slight increase in cleft palate amongst the offspring of mothers treated with this group of drugs. There may, of course, be circumstances when adrenal steroids are needed for pregnant women, but they must only be administered by the patient's physician after due consideration.

It has been suggested that congenital deformities in the fetus may result from the administration of A.S.A. tablets, antacids, amphetamines, phenobarbitone, sodium amytal and other barbiturates, iron, and sulphonamides. It has also been suggested, though not confirmed, that a maternal deficiency of ascorbic and folic acids may produce deformities. In this whole area there are many suggestions but not many hard facts.

While we are on the subject of reproductive or prenatal deformities, we should remember that the best-known example of deformity of the fetus is that caused by rubella or German measles. The German measles virus can cause cataracts, deafness, mental defects, and congenital heart disease. The earlier this infection occurs during pregnancy, the more damage is done to the fetus. It is thought that viruses such as cytomegalovirus may cause damage to the fetus, and damage can be caused by *Toxoplasma gondii,* a small parasite. It has also been suggested that polio virus, influenza virus, and *Herpes virus hominis* may be teratogenic in humans. The evidence, however, is inconclusive.

Dietary Supplements in Pregnancy

In general, dietary supplements are not necessary in pregnancy, with the exception of iron and folic acid in reasonable doses. If the pregnant women is eating a good diet, she will need neither dietary supplements nor drugs. Obviously, if she is suffering from a disease, it will be necessary for her physician to decide which drugs she needs.

Treatment of Illnesses

Constipation and indigestion are two common problems accompanying pregnancy. Laxatives are best avoided. Mineral oil dissolves the fat-soluble vitamins A, D, and K, thus preventing their absorption by the body. Other laxatives may produce a depletion of potassium, and sodium as well. Certain antacids may interfere with iron absorption and cause an excessive excretion of phosphate. There are a remarkable number of interactions between drugs and nutrients, many of which are not generally known. For instance, the anti-convulsant drugs such as phenytoin and phenobarbital may produce a folate deficiency or a vitamin D deficiency, which may in turn result in megaloblastic anemia. It is well to be aware of this sort of interaction before taking or prescribing medicinal drugs, in pregnancy or otherwise.

Obstetrical Medication

One of the most serious concerns for the fetus is adequate oxygen supply. The supply of oxygen may be restricted by a number of things—a defect in the placenta; bleeding behind the placenta; labor that is too long; prolapse of the umbilical cord; wrong presentation of the fetus; a gestation that has gone on too long; and heavy maternal sedation during labor. Some or all of these conditions may result in fetal distress, which the obstetrician or physician will detect. A general anesthetic during labor may also contribute to a lack of oxygen in the fetus, which may have damaging effects on the infant's nervous system.

Obstetrical medications—those given to women during labor and delivery—appear to have long-lasting effects on childrens' behavior. Dr. Yvonne Brackbill and colleagues of the University of Florida have estimated that women are given medications in 95 per cent of labors and deliveries in the United States. She and Dr. Sarah Broman, of the National Institute of Neurological and Communicative Disorders and Stroke, have studied data on 3500 healthy full-term babies born to women who participated in the Collaborative Perinatal Project, a longitudinal study of more than 50,000 infants overseen by the National Institute of Health in the 1950s. These two behavioral psychologists believe that obstetric medication affected the childrens' behavior at least through seven years of age. Children of mothers heavily medicated, tested at four months, eight months, and one year, lagged in the development of the ability to sit, to stand, and to move about. As they grew older, their development of language and cognitive skills lagged or was impaired.

Other drugs that affect infant and child behavior when taken in pregnancy are the narcotics, including methadone and heroin. Infants of addicted mothers have been studied by Dr. Donald Hutchings of the New York State Psychiatric Institute. They are difficult to live with because their behavior is disturbed. As Hutchings points out, "No foster parents can tolerate these babies and they bounce from one foster home to the next." They have voracious appetites, yet they fail to gain weight, and later on they tend to be hyperactive and to have short attention spans. These situations give us pause for thought about the use of analgesics and narcotics in obstetrics. Obviously there are many situations when these drugs are necessary, but one wonders whether they are too routinely used. Natural childbirth seems to be preferable by far to the usual North American obstetrical procedure, which makes a surgical operation out of what should be a natural process.

Other Chemicals

It is clear that the pregnant woman should do her best to stay away from any new or doubtful chemicals. If she lives on a farm, for example, she should not come into contact with pesticides even if it is proven that pesticides are not pathogens. What evidence we have is that, in general, pesticides are not teratogenic in humans in the usual degree of exposure to them. But that does not mean that we should become complacent about them or treat them casually. Where the fetus is concerned, it is better to be safe than sorry.

We do not really know what levels of various pesticides in mothers' milk are acceptable and which levels are dangerous. For obvious reasons, we cannot do experiments on infants, and animal experiments are not necessarily applicable to the human situation. Mothers' milk, as far as possible, shouldn't contain noxious chemicals, which is a counsel of perfection.

Polychlorinated biphenyls are still in use in North America, although their use is much restricted. PCBs have been detected in the study of human milk in Colorado, where eight of 40 samples obtained had residues ranging from 40 to 100 parts per billion. In Ontario these residues were found to be approximately 1 mg/kg on a fat basis. We do not know whether these amounts of this chemical are harmful or not. The amounts found are very small indeed, and they have only been found because of modern, very accurate methods of scientific chemical detection. As far as we know, the infants who have ingested these substances are healthy. Only the future will tell whether they have been damaged.

Lest the foregoing discussion lead to panic, we should bear in mind that over the ages, long before we knew about the effects of chemicals in the environment, mothers and infants have been exposed to a wide variety of noxious substances— chemical, viral, and bacterial. The human is a very resistant animal. The body can adjust to a remarkable number of noxious substances. Human populations in North America have been exposed to a wide range of pesticides for the past 25 years. By whatever evidence we have, we have not been able to detect any carcinogenic, teratogenic, or mutagenic effects in humans from these substances. Obviously, the situation might change, but so far conscientious and improved testing methods are keeping serious poisons off the market and out of the environment.

Alcohol and the Fetus

We have known since 1968 that alcohol is teratogenic and that it damages the fetus. As a result of extensive animal studies it has been shown that ethyl alcohol is a teratogen in animals, including humans. Alcohol has remained the common denominator in the case histories of a large number of pregnant women, and it is known to have produced abnormal offspring. These deformed children have been found in the United States, in Germany, and indeed all over the world.

The effects of alcohol on the fetus show a broad range of abnormalities, ranging from mild to moderate retardation, microcephaly or a very small brain, poor co-ordination, irritability in infancy, hyperactivity in childhood, disproportionately diminished adipose (fatty) tissue, and specific facial characteristics: Short eyelid fissures, a short, upturned nose, typical marking of the upper lip. Mental retardation is one of the commonest and most serious problems in such cases. With the knowledge of the risks involved, surely no woman would consume alcohol while she is pregnant.

Cigaret Smoking

From the most recent Surgeon General's Report on Smoking and Health, it is quite clear that cigaret smoking during pregnancy has a deleterious effect on the fetus, on the newborn, and on the future development of the infant and child. Mothers who smoke heavily have more spontaneous abortions or fetal deaths, preterm births, and neonatal deaths. They also experience more retardation in fetal growth, their children are smaller than average, and there are numerous problems of adaptation in the neonatal period. There are long-term impairments in physical growth, diminished intellectual function, and deficiency in behavioral development in infants who survive the first four weeks of life. The children of smoking mothers do not catch up with the offspring of non-smoking mothers in various phases of development.

It should be quite clear that smoking during pregnancy is harmful, not only to the mother, but also to the fetus and the infant. Studies carried out in Ontario showed that women who smoked during pregnancy had excess fetal deaths that were unexplained or anoxia deaths close to birth due to premature delivery. Many conditions, like placenta previa, bleeding at or after confinement, and early rupture of the membranes are more common in mothers who smoke heavily. Breast-fed infants of such mothers can suffer from nicotine poisoning, with symptoms including restlessness, vomiting, diarrhea, and rapid heartbeat. The symptoms stop when the mother stops smoking.

For pregnant women, the choice is clear. Chemicals, including alcohol and tobacco, are to be avoided. Medicinal drugs are not indicated for use by the healthy pregnant woman; they should be used only when absolutely necessary.

9.

Do Foods Cause Cancer?

Nowadays we all expect to live beyond the age of 70, and we do not expect to die from an infectious disease—such diseases have been virtually eliminated in North America. But we will surely die of something. Chief causes of death today are, in order of importance:

1. all the vascular diseases—heart disease, cerebrovascular diseases, and others in this group account for something like half of all deaths, most of them in people over the age of 65.
2. various forms of cancer, accounting for about 20 per cent of deaths.
3. accidents and violence—automobile accidents cause about 10 per cent of all deaths.

The relatively small number of deaths left over are due to respiratory diseases, infant mortality, and congenital abnormalities, with about one per cent due to infectious diseases.

This list should help us to consider cancer a bit more objectively. Although it is a very important cause of death, it is not first on the list. During the last few years the impression has been created that there has been a vast increase in the number of deaths from cancer. Not true. If, for instance, we look at the age standardized mortality rates in Canada from 1966 to 1978, and if we look at all cancers in males, we see an increase in the rate of about 149 per 100,000 to about 163

per 100,000. If from these figures we subtract lung cancer, we
find there has been a *decrease* in death rates from cancer from
about 116 to 112 per 100,000. This means that in males the
prime cause of death from cancer is lung cancer. As a matter
of fact, one third of all cancer deaths in males are due to cancer
in the lung, and it has been well established that most cases of
lung cancer result from cigaret smoking. Cancer death rates for
females in the same period have remained approximately
constant, and if we subtract lung cancer from these statistics,
there is also a substantial drop in cancer deaths in females.
Women in Canada and elsewhere are now also doing their best
to die from lung cancer, because more of them appear to be
smoking. The latent period for lung cancer is in the region of
20 years or more. This means that it takes at least 20 years to
see a change in rates when people either start or stop smoking
in large numbers.

The point to remember about cancer is this: Although it
is a very serious group of diseases, there is no need to think
that there is a tremendous increase in cancer death rates in
North America.

Data prepared by the American Cancer Society indicate
the rates of occurrence of various types of cancer in males and
females. In males in the United States, the commonest cause
of death from cancer is cancer of the lung, followed by cancer
of the prostate. In females 26 per cent of all cancer deaths are
due to cancer of the breast, and 15 per cent are due to cancer
of the colon and rectum. We do not know for sure what causes
either of these types of cancer.

In the period between 1930 and 1975 in the United States
in males the spectacular increase in death rates from cancer
has been in lung cancer. There is no doubt that this is a real
increase and that several of the causes are known: Cigaret
smoking, air pollution, and occupational exposures. At the
same time there has been a considerable decrease in mortality
from cancer of the stomach. The reasons are unknown—perhaps
purer, cleaner, and better food is a contributing factor. During
the same period there has been a decrease in the death rate in
males from liver cancer, but an increase in mortality from
leukemia. This is almost certainly partially due to an improve-

ment in diagnosis, but some of it is possibly due to the increase in ionizing radiation, mainly from therapeutic x-rays. We do not know why there has been a modest increase in the death rate from cancer of the pancreas, which is a difficult condition to diagnose.

In females there has been a marked increase in death from lung cancer, no doubt reflecting the increase in smoking. In breast cancer, a very serious cancer in women, the rates remained more or less stable for half a century, although there has been a slight increase in the last 10 years. A disturbing conclusion in connection with breast cancer is that whatever we have done in treating this disease has not influenced death rates. Deaths from cancer of the uterus have been declining, while the death rates for cancer of the ovary have been slowly increasing. Why? We don't know.

In Canada statistics show that lung cancer was the leading site in men, breast cancer in women. Cancer statistics for Canada between 1931 and 1974 show the following:

Rapid increase: Lung

Moderate increases: Pancreas, brain, lymphatic tissue, leukemia (males)

Relatively constant: Large intestine minus rectum (males), rectum (males), breast (females), prostate, bladder (males), leukemia (females)

Moderate decreases: Buccal cavity and pharynx, large intestine minus rectum (females), rectum (females), gallbladder, cervix, bladder (females)

Rapid decreases: Stomach, uterus

What Is Cancer?

Each case of cancer starts out as a defect in one of our cells. This cell then starts multiplying, giving rise to a population of similar cells which are unrestricted in their growh and which invade other tissues. If the cells are in the skin, the growth will usually be detected; if they are in the lung, detection will take some time. If they are in the breast a lump can be found. In other words, some kinds of cancer can be relatively easily detected; others, in the hidden recesses of the body, are not easily discovered.

If the cancer is found quickly, the growth can be removed surgically. If not, it may send some of its cancerous cells to other parts of the body, where they may form new colonies, known as metastases. For instance, if a person has a carcinoma of the lung these metastses may migrate to, say, the liver. Obviously, when this has happened removal of the tumor in the lung will not influence the tumor cells in the liver. At that point, other forms of treatment may be necessary, such as radiation or drugs.

We should remember that some growths are benign—they merely enlarge and do not invade. It is sometimes difficult for the pathologist to decide whether the cells he is examining under a microscope are benign or malignant. Pathologists are also fallible human beings, and mistakes are possible.

During the last few years it has become almost axiomatic that the public assume that all cancers are due to poisons in the environment. This is not true. There are poisons in the environment and they can cause cancer, but the matter is not quite that simple. We do know that certain chemicals cause cancer or are involved in the production of cancer. The first two pure carcinogens to be identified were derived from tar: dibenz (a,h) anthracene and benz (a) pyrene. The first cancer was induced experimentally in 1915 by applying tar repeatedly to the ears of rabbits over a period of many months. (It takes a long time for cancer to be produced by external agents.) Apart from chemicals, other ways of producing cancer have been through various types of radiation, including x-rays and fallout from nuclear bombs.

In some cases of cancer we can determine the cause—for example, when people have been exposed, particularly in an industrial setting, to certain carcinogenic chemicals. And, of course, we know that tobacco smoke is a very effective carcinogen. It is very clear that cigaret smoking can produce cancer of the lung, larynx, bladder, lip, tongue, tonsil, mouth, and pharynx, and it is probably associated with some cancers of the esophagus, kidney, and pancreas. Pipe smokers have a larger incidence of cancer in the oral cavity and in the larynx; chewing tobacco, too, can produce cancers in the oral cavity.

Not everybody gets cancer from a carcinogen. Some people are more resistent than others. As an analogy, if people drink water containing typhoid bacilli, unless the dose is extremely large, only a certain proportion of them become ill. The question of dosage also applies in the production of cancer in humans or in experimental animals. Certain occupations are obviously dangerous because of chronic exposure to certain carcinogenic agents in the places of work; for instance, pesticide workers may be poisoned by arsenic, certain industrial workers may be affected by vinyl chloride. In the old days in England, chimney sweeps were affected by the products of coal or tar, many of them developing cancer of the scrotum.

Ionizing radiation may be carcinogenic. Ultraviolet light, particularly in people with fair skins, may produce skin cancer. Asbestos, particularly associated with cigaret smoking, produces lung cancer and possibly cancer in other parts of the body. Every effort should be made in industry to ventilate and to get rid of the carcinogens. We should note, however, that the types of cancer from which people die in general are not industrially produced. Most cases of cancer at present result from unknown causes. In the final analysis, some of these causes must be chemical, but we do not know what they are.

Geographical Differences in Cancer Incidence

It is most interesting that the prevalence of different types of cancer varies in different parts of the world. The reasons for this can only be advanced as educated guesses. Environmental circumstances; different diets; and possibly, in a few cases, genetic predisposition or resistance. Some years ago two research workers in Japan, Professors Mitsuo Segi and Minoru Kurihara, produced some important data on cancer mortality in different parts of the world. Twenty-four countries were studied, and some of these results are fascinating, if puzzling. For instance, according to those figures, the highest age-adjusted death rates for malignant cancers of the mouth and pharynx for males were in France and the lowest in Japan. The French males also had a very high incidence of cancer of the esophagus. We could speculate that cigaret smoking and alcohol consumption contribute to these cancers. The point then would be actually to examine whether French men smoke and drink much more than do Japanese men. We don't know. In cancer of the stomach, Japanese males lead; white American males have the fewest deaths of cancer of the stomach. In females the top of the list for cancers of the intestine, except rectum, are Scotland, and lowest Japan. Is this a result of diet? Heredity? Why do Danish males have a death rate from cancer of the rectum twice as high as Danish females? We don't know. In cancers of the liver and urinary passages we find high rates in Japanese males and Israeli females. New Zealand males have the distinction of having the highest death rate from cancer of the pancreas, while Japanese males have the lowest rate. French males have a death rate of 10 per 100,000 for cancer of the larynx, while Swedish males have a rate of less than 1 per 100,000 for the same disease. Of the 24 countries studied, the highest rate of cancer of the lung and trachea in men was Scotland, in Scottish males, the lowest rate in Portugal. In females the highest rate for deaths from cancer of the breast was in Denmark, with the lowest rate in Japan. One of the suggested explanations here is that there is more breast feeding in Japan.

All these figures merely serve to illustrate that much is not known about the causes of cancer, despite the pontification in many places on this subject. For instance, the fact that Japanese males have the lowest rate for breast cancer as well as Japanese females makes one wonder about the breast-feeding hypothesis.

Cancer is not just one disease—it is a complex group of diseases. The etiology—the cause—of cancer involves many factors. For one thing, the incidence rates are different in males and females. There are variations by geography, which may be influenced not only by genetic composition but also by environmental circumstances. Death rates from cancer vary within countries, so that there are different rates in different parts of the United States and in Canada. Cancer is related to certain chemical agents, and it is most probably related to hormones, particularly the sex hormones; it may also be related to diet and to alcohol. Furthermore, humans breathe air that contains various contaminants; there is every chance that air pollution may influence certain types of cancer. Then again there are physical agents such as sunshine. We know that highest rates of skin cancer are found in blonds in South Africa and in Australia. Then there are various effects of radiation, from medical use of radiation to occupational exposures in radiologists.

Many biological agents may produce cancer, particularly various types of virus. The Epstein-Barr virus is suspected of being one of the causes of Burkitt's tumor, a cancer that occurs mainly amongst children in certain areas of Africa with elevations below 1800 m, average temperature above 16°C, and where annual rainfall exceeds 60 cm. It has also been thought that there may be a virus etiology of breast cancer, leukemia, sarcomas, and other tumors, although none of this has been proven. Infestation with the parasite, *Schistosoma haematobium,* increases the risk of bladder cancer, particularly in Egypt.

The group of diseases we call cancer represents a large variety of pathological conditions; it is probably started by a number of different agents acting over a period of time, and it is highly probable that two or three agents in concert may be involved in starting certain cancers. For instance, chemical agents, viruses, and hormones may co-operate in particular circumstances in particular places and in particular sexes. It could well be that there is also a genetic element in cancer.

Two of the most interesting groups who have been studied are the Mormons in the United States and the Seventh Day Adventists, who live mainly in North America but also in other countries like Australia. Studies of these groups have produced fascinating results. Members of the Church of Jesus Christ of the Latter Day Saints, commonly called the Mormons, have proscribed the use of alcohol, tobacco, coffee, and tea in all forms for health reasons for at least 80 years. Furthermore, the church teaches strong family attachments, high educational attainments, and stringent sexual morals, forbidding premarital and extramarital sexual intercourse for both men and women.

Dr. Joseph Lyon, Dr. John W. Gardiner, and D. W. West from the Department of Family and Community Medicine, University of Utah College of Medicine, Salt Lake City, have found that Mormons have a considerably lower cancer death rate than non-Mormons in Utah. Especially low in death rates are the cancer sites associated with cigaret smoking—lung, larynx, esophagus, and bladder. Here we have what might be called a natural experiment, and the results are obvious. It is also interesting that in Mormons there are lower death rates for cancers of the colon and stomach than in non-Mormons, and fewer cases of cancer of the female breast. And in addition, Mormon women had far fewer cases of cancer of the cervix than did non-Mormons. This phenomenon may be related to sexual practice; Mormons are restrained in their sexual activities and opposed to promiscuity. On the other hand, cancer of the lip, prostate, and skin show an incidence significantly above the United States expectations. Why, we don't know.

Among Mormons in California, a 35-year-old active Mormon has about an 11 per cent chance of dying before the age of 65; a similar 35-year-old average U.S. white male has a 30 per cent chance of dying before the age of 65. Also at age 35 an active California Mormon male has a remaining life expectancy of 44.6 years, about eight years greater than for the United States as a whole.

How do Mormons differ from the rest of the U.S. population? There is no clear difference between Mormons and other U.S. whites in the use of eggs, fruits, vegetables, desserts, and whole milk, but it appears that Mormons use somewhat less meat, fish, or poultry. California Mormons consume a large amount of vitamin supplements; it would be interesting to test whether this has a favorable effect in the Mormon experience in relation to cancer. The major differences can be summarized as follows: Active Mormons use essentially no cigarets, cigars, pipes, beer, wine, liquor, coffee, or tea. They have a higher educational level and most marry and have a large number of children. Mormon men tend to have a higher occupational level than the national average, and most of the women are housewives and homemakers. Active Mormons drink more milk, use more fruits and vegetables and vitamin and mineral supplements; they have sound health practices; and they have more frequent medical check-ups. They have a lower mean blood cholesterol level. They do not differ significantly from the general population in regard to participation in active sports, physical exercise, the use of non-prescription drugs, total intake of calories and fat, intake of vitamins and minerals for foods and intake of dietary cholesterol. But their differences may be significant, and there may be some lessons to be learned from them.

Another very interesting group are the Seventh Day Adventists, who have followed their unique lifestyle for about 100 years. They abstain from all types of smoking and alcoholic beverages, and 50 per cent of them follow a lacto-ovo vegetarian diet. They also tend to avoid coffee, tea, and other caffeine-containing beverages, which include cocoa and cola. They also do not eat rich, highly refined foods, and they do not use hot condiments and spices. There is no doubt that the people who belong to the Seventh Day Adventist Group are highly selected; some of them have been born into the community, others have chosen to become members of it. To the purist in experimentation there are some questions to be asked about the experimental design, but as a natural experiment it supports the contention that lifestyle affects health, specifically where cancer is concerned. Studies of this group in California have shown that the risk of fatal cancer amongst Adventist males is 53 per cent of the risk amongst all U.S. white males of comparable age. For Adventist females the risk is 68 per cent of the rest of all U.S. white females. For both sexes combined the Adventist compared with the United States mortality ratios are significantly low for all causes of death, as well as all the cancer sites shown, except for breast, prostate, and lymphomas. The low risk amongst Adventists as compared to all U.S. whites is particularly pronounced for lung cancer and other smoking-related cancer sites among males, clearly a reflection of the Adventists' abstinence from tobacco. Among the sites that are unrelated to smoking, colon and rectal cancer was the site of lowest risk amongst Adventists for both men and women; also for both sexes, rates of stomach cancer and leukemia were significantly lower than for the U.S. population as a whole. It cannot be absolutely proven, but one could suggest that the low colon-rectal cancer risk amongst Adventists is due to dietary habits; the Adventist diet is vegetarian, with a high roughage content.

Cancer and the Total Environment

As far back as 1968 Dr. John Higginson made the estimate that between 80 and 90 per cent of all cancers were causally related to environmental factors. This was interpreted by the news media and by some political pressure groups to mean that pollutants and chemical substances in the workplace are the major causes of cancer. In a subsequent discussion with Thomas H. Maugh III, published in *Science* Magazine, he pointed out that the 1968 statement included the *total* environment, cultural as well as chemical and environmental. In other words, a considerable proportion of cancers are related to tobacco or tobacco and alcohol, to sunlight exposures, to diet, and to lifestyle, such as sexual lifestyle. A relatively small proportion of cancers, he estimated, were due to exposure in occupation. It is quite obvious that we should look at the total environment in looking for causes of cancer. It is unwise and unbalanced to try to attribute cancer to one single cause or group of causes and then start a campaign in that direction.

Diet may well be a factor in a number of cancers. For example, the lower incidence of gastrointestinal cancers among Utah Mormons might be attributed to dietary practices. Mormons eat meat sparingly and lots of fruits, vegetables, and whole grains. There is some evidence that vitamin C, ascorbic acid, may inhibit the synthesis of carcinogenic N-nitroso compounds from nitrites and related substances and that it might also inhibit intracolonic synthesis of mutagens in people on high fat and protein diets. Some of this work has been done by Dr. W. R. Bruce in Toronto. It also has been found that vitamin A may inhibit the actions of carcinogens on the trachea, bronchus, lungs, skin, mammary gland, cervix, urinary bladder, and colon. Furthermore, there is some evidence that vitamin E, which is a potent antioxidant, also has an inhibitory effect on the intracolonic synthesis of mutagens thought to be N-nitroso compounds. There is also evidence, at least in rat experiments, that a carcinogen-detoxifying enzyme is greatly enhanced by the feeding of cabbage, Brussels sprouts, cauliflower, and turnips. So it may well be that these vegetables have an anti-carcinogenic effect quite separate from the other qualities they possess.

There is suggested evidence that Mormon males have a low incidence of stomach cancer because of high quantities of vitamins C and A in their foods. The evidence is growing that nutrition is important in the prevention of at least certain carcinogens, although it is very hard to prove this unequivocally in humans. We can only repeat that there are many causes of cancer and that when we study the effects of the production of cancer in humans we should study the total environment, not just one set of observations. There may for example, be trace elements in the soil, the water, or the vegetation in Utah that may inhibit carcinogens. In recent laboratory studies it has been suggested that selenium may have an anti-carcinogenic effect. It has been shown that the development of spontaneous breast cancer and carcinogen-induced colon cancer can be inhibited by administration of selenium. But before we get too excited and start taking selenium pills, we should know that too much selenium causes liver damage. Animals receiving large doses of selenium may die of liver failure. If people take or are given selenium, the amounts must be very small, no more than the adequate daily intakes recommended by the Food and Nutrition Board of the National Academy of Sciences—0.2 mg per day.

From the epidemiological studies of differing cancer death rates in different parts of the world, epidemiologists are developing hypotheses about the causes of cancer that can then be tested out in the laboratory on experimental animals. Animal experimentation is the main stage of our fight against disease in general and cancer in particular, for it is extremely difficult, if not impossible, to carry out dietary modification experiments on humans that will run over a long period. That is why it is so revealing to study natural experiments, such as the very interesting finding of superior health in the Mormon and Adventist communities.

Further Epidemiologic Observations on Populations

In addition to the Mormon and Adventist communities, other natural experiments exist. For instance, there are many interesting observations to be derived from migrant populations. For the Japanese population in Japan, the incidence of colon and breast cancer is low, stomach cancer high. The reverse is true of the United States population. However, when Japanese move to the United States, by the third generation there is a shift of cancer incidence patterns from those common in Japan to those prevalent in the United States. This means that Japanese who have been living in the United States for three generations develop the same types of cancer as the rest of the American population. This is very strong evidence suggesting that foods are important in the production of cancer. Of course it can be said that air pollution and smoking may also be involved, but smoking and air pollution do not differ very much in the United States and many parts of Japan. If the carcinogenic substances in smoking had a role in the production of cancer of the colon, breast, stomach, and some other forms of cancer, then one would expect that these types of cancer would be common among smokers. But they aren't.

Changes also take place within the same population. For instance, during the last 10 years in Japan, stomach cancer rates have gone down and colon cancer rates have gone up. The decrease in stomach cancer might be because the Japanese are now drinking more milk and eating more raw vegetables. On the other hand, they are also eating more meat, such as beef, and more fat, and there is a great deal of suggestive evidence that fat, particularly beef fat, is related in some way to colon cancer. It is not clear whether the causal factor is the meat itself or the fat itself or a relative lack of fiber and roughage. We should remember that the Western world, where there is a higher intake of meat and fat, is a constipated world, and it is in this setting that there is a greater incidence of cancer of the colon. Mortality rates from cancer of the colon are high in the United States, Scotland, and Canada, which are high meat-consuming countries. In other populations, such as Japan and

Chile, with low meat consumption, there is a low incidence of colon cancer. We have already pointed out that Seventh Day Adventists and Mormons have a restricted fat and meat intake and they suffer considerably less from some forms of cancer, notably that of breast and colon.

In regard to the fat hypothesis and cancer of the colon, an interesting critique has recently been written by Mary E. Enig and associates, who have analyzed the types of fat in relation to cancer of the colon and breast cancer. What these workers have found is that there is a significant positive correlation for total fat and either a negative or no correlation with animal fat. This is an interesting point, in that it suggests that some of the modern, chemically processed, hydrogenated fats and margarines may contain "trans" fatty acids, which have been found to render cell membranes more permeable to carcinogens. If these fats are given to animals the cellular membranes change so that the cells more readily admit carcinogens. This opens up a fascinating area for research, as it suggests that the manipulated vegetable fats may be harmful and that we should eat natural fats, whether animal or vegetable, that have not been chemically altered.

Cancer of the Esophagus

Many case control studies have shown a considerable increase of cancer of the upper alimentary tract—including mouth, throat, tongue, and larynx—in people who consume large amounts of alcohol in association or in conjunction with cigaret smoking. The relationship of alcohol to cancer of the esophagus is not clear. There are many areas in the world, such as on the border of the Caspian Sea in Iran, where there is a very high incidence of cancer of the esophagus. These people do not drink much alcohol, but their diet is very deficient, consisting mainly of bread and tea and virtually no fresh fruit or vegetables. The potential carcinogens for these people come from opium, sesame oil in cooking, chewing tobacco, preservation of meat by salting and drying, and the use of underground storage pits lined with straw for grain storage. However, a specific carcinogen has not been found in Iran. In certain parts of Africa and in Mozambique, there are also groups of people with high incidences of esophageal cancer. This is almost certainly related to some type of food or poison in the food, probably a mold or fungal growth. Similar evidence comes from China. There is no doubt that factors surrounding the development of esophageal cancer vary in different parts of the world. The cancer may be the result of a combination of factors, perhaps a toxin, probably from a fungus, combined with a number of nutritional deficiencies, particularly deficiencies of vitamins A and C.

Cancer of the Stomach

It is interesting that the highest rates of cancer of the stomach are in Japan, Eastern Russia, Iceland, Chile, Poland, and Finland; rates are much lower in the United States, Australia, Uganda, and Canada. Since 1930 there has been a remarkable decline in deaths from cancer of the stomach in the United States and Canada. And although the rates are high in Japan, during the last 10 years there has also been a decline there in deaths from cancer of the stomach. This all suggests environmental factors in this disease, and especially nutritional factors. Dr. Toshio Oiso of the International Institute of Nutrition in Tokyo has suggested that cancer of the stomach in Japan is possibly related to a very hot rice gruel and also the consumption of salty food such as soybean paste, soya bean sauce, salted pickles and small fish, and shellfish or seaweed boiled with soybean sauce, which are eaten as side dishes to complement boiled white rice. The Japanese also like to eat fish that is broiled until it is black. It has been assumed that carcinogens are present in some of these foods. He also suggests that sake, which contains 15 to 16 percent alcohol and which is drunk warm, may be a factor. However, an interesting dietary change in Japan since 1949 is the growth in milk, egg, meat, and poultry consumption. This may have influenced the decrease in a number of cases of stomach cancer.

There is evidence that nitrates may have an influence not only on stomach cancer, but cancer of the intestine. It should be remembered, though, that nitrates occur naturally in many foods, principally in vegetables and drinking water, as well as in preserved meats. In fact, most of the nitrites derived from nitrates come from vegetables and, in some instances, drinking water; areas with high nitrate levels in drinking water have an abnormally high death rate for gastric cancer. It has also been shown that nitrate concentrations in the human stomach rise considerably as the level of acidity in the stomach approaches neutrality. Thus people who have a naturally neutral gastric acid level may be more susceptible to the risk of gastric cancer. It has been found that patients with pernicious anemia, who have an increased risk of gastric cancer, in fact have a 50-fold greater nitrate concentration in the stomach than healthy people of the same age. It has been suggested that gastric cancer is associated with a predominantly starchy diet, void of fat, fresh fruit, and vegetables. An association can also be shown with food preserved by salting or pickling. A significant risk has also been found in cigaret smokers, but some protection is afforded them from drinking over two glasses of milk a day.

Cancer of the Pancreas

Cancer of the pancreas seems to be increasing in many western countries, although part of this measured increase is due to better diagnosis. The people who have the highest incidence rates for this cancer are New Zealand Maoris, native Hawaiians, and United States non-whites. It is more common in men than in women. It seems to be related to dietary fat intake and cigaret smoking, and some workers have found an association with protein intake, but it is not clear how these factors lead to pancreatic cancer. It should be pointed out that the risk in cigaret smokers is about double that in the general population, and the risk is directly related to the amount smoked; smokers get pancreatic cancer 10 to 15 years earlier than non-smokers.

The association with smoking probably explains the predominance of this cancer in males. Cancer of the pancreas, then, in many instances is related to toxic substances derived from cigaret smoking and also possibly toxic substances from the diet, although the latter situation is by no means clear.

Cancer of the Colon

Cancer of the colon, or large bowel, which is a relatively common condition in western countries, may well have a dietary origin. It is a disease of developed or industrialized countries, being most prevalent in Scotland, the United States of America, New Zealand, and Denmark. It is uncommon in Africa and South America, with the exception of Argentina, where people eat a great deal of meat—beef. Males and females are affected equally, except for rectal cancer, where males predominate. The fact that the incidence of rectal cancer is declining while that of colon cancer is rising has led to the suggestion that rectal cancer has a separate etiology from other large bowel tumors.

Bile acids are considered to be co-carcinogens. We know that bile acids are normally present in the gut, but it has been shown that their concentration is much higher in the feces of subjects living in high bowel cancer incidence areas like the United States and Britain and low in Japanese and Ugandan stools. Patients with colon cancer have significantly higher fecal bile acid levels than matched controls. Dietary fat fits into this hypothesis as well, since increasing animal fat intake leads to a pronounced increase in fecal bile acid secretion. From a number of studies it appears that there is a clear association between animal fat intake and bowel cancer, although this is not invariable. There seems to be some relation to protein, and some people think it is related to beef in particular. Dietary fiber, or lack of it, has also been implicated, the theory being that the dietary fiber dilutes the carcinogens that are thought to be produced in a high fat and possible high protein diet. It may be that fiber also affects colonic bacterial metabolism. It is possible that it is fat plus lack of fiber that is the main influence in producing cancer of the colon. Recent animal studies have shown that high protein diets increase colon tumor formation, and it has been suggested that bacterial protein metabolites, such as ammonia, phenyl cresol, and tryptophane metabolites, are themselves promoters of tumors.

Breast Cancer and Diet

There is a general impression that breast cancer, as well as cancer of the colon, appears to be associated with a diet high in fat, particularly animal fat. The exact mechanism of this is not known. Case control studies have also shown a relationship between breast cancer and the age at first pregnancy and family history. These studies have not reported any particular variables that, for instance, would account for a major difference in U.S.—Japanese breast cancer rates, differences for increased rates amongst post-menopausal women, the increased breast cancer rate amongst Japanese migrants, and a current increase in breast cancer in Japan itself. It has been known for a long time, particularly from the work of Tannenbaum, that dietary fats significantly increase the growth of both spontaneous and induced breast cancer in animals. It appears that plasma prolactin is significantly elevated in women consuming a high fat diet. In addition, women who have first pregnancies late in life have a high daytime serum prolactin level. This finding may account for the reported high risk of breast cancer, and may be related to anovulation and sub-fertility.

It is interesting that breast fluid secretion is reported to be less common among Orientals than in white women. The breast fluid is in intimate contact with the ductal glands or mammary glands. It has been found the prolactin and estrogen levels are greater in the fluid than in the serum. It has also been found that with advanced age, the serum prolactin levels increase slightly while the estrogen levels decrease, therefore increasing the prolactin/estrogen ratio. It may be significant that nicotine can be found in breast fluid. Recently it has been shown that nicotine appeared in the breast fluid within five minutes after smoking. This raises the possibility that cigaret smoking may also be associated with breast cancer.

Family Studies in Cancer

It should be remembered that there is a genetic component of
varying intensity in different types of cancer. From the variety
of studies that have been done, it appears that there is a familial
tendency to cancer in the female breast, stomach, colon, prostate, lung, and cervix. This means that certain people may
have a genetic predisposition to these cancers, which are then
acted upon by various chemical and hormonal agents. We can
do nothing about our heredity, but we certainly can do a great
deal about the food we eat.

A Diet to Minimize the Risk of Cancer

If we look at the diets of the Mormons and Seventh Day Adventists we will note that they either eat very little meat, and in
fact some of them are vegetarians. So we might conclude that
a reduction in meat intake would be an advantage. Less meat,
particularly beef, which has been implicated in several studies,
and probably more fish and poultry. In addition, Seventh Day
Adventists do not smoke, they do not drink alcohol, and they
do not drink coffee, tea, cocoa, or other caffeine-containing
beverages. There may be an advantage to this dietary custom.
In addition, they are encouraged to eat a great deal of fresh
fruit and vegetables as well as whole grains. It could be that
this type of diet, containing modest amounts of animal fat with
adequate supplies of eggs, vegetables, and fruit, could be
regarded as the diet that will make for the greatest degree of
good health. Whether additional supplies of vitamin A and
anti-oxidant vitamins such as C and E should be taken is not
yet clear, but there are some suggestions that it would be useful
in people who have a great deal of nitrosamines in their stools.
This may prevent cancer of the colon. On the other hand, one
would not suggest large doses of vitamins because by chance
they might prevent cancer. We know for certain that overdosage
of vitamins A and D can undoubtedly be deleterious, but we

do not know what overdoses *are* for the B vitamins and what many of the others will do. This is so far an uncharted sea, and it will be interesting in the future to find out whether large doses of these vitamins will be useful or not.

We have discussed at some length those factors that may be involved in the production of cancer, with specific reference to carcinogens in food. Note that all the substances we have discussed are found as natural constituents of foods.

FIGURE 9:1

† RELATIVE FREQUENCY OF SELECTED CANCER SITES BY SEX.

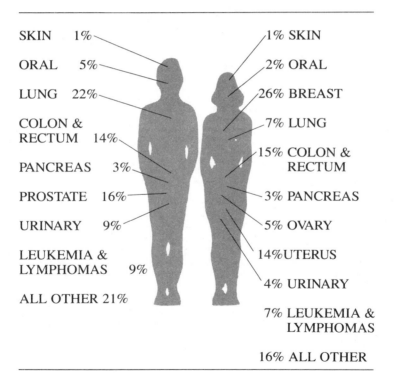

SKIN 1%	1% SKIN
ORAL 5%	2% ORAL
LUNG 22%	26% BREAST
COLON & RECTUM 14%	7% LUNG
PANCREAS 3%	15% COLON & RECTUM
PROSTATE 16%	3% PANCREAS
URINARY 9%	5% OVARY
LEUKEMIA & LYMPHOMAS 9%	14% UTERUS
ALL OTHER 21%	4% URINARY
	7% LEUKEMIA & LYMPHOMAS
	16% ALL OTHER

†Excluding non-melanoma skin cancer and carcinoma in situ of uterine cervix.

10.

Atherosclerosis, Heart Disease, and Diet

The diseases that kill people today are quite different from those that killed them years ago. Take, for example, the causes of death in Ontario in the year 1900. First on the list was tuberculosis, then respiratory diseases—pneumonia and influenza; third on the list was senility, which obviously is not a very diagnostic term. As we mentioned in the chapter on cancer, today's foremost killers are, first, heart disease and diseases of the circulatory system; second, cancer; and third, accidents and violence. The discovery of antibiotics and sulphonamides had a profound effect on infectious diseases—they still exist, but they are no longer major killers. At present in most western countries, for every 1000 people there will be 10 deaths in a given year. In some communities there will be fewer deaths, but 10 is a reasonable number. Of these 10 deaths, five will be from cardiovascular causes—heart disease, cerebrovascular diseases, strokes, and so forth—and of these five, four people will be over the age of 65. This is important: Even if we say that 50 per cent of all deaths are due to cardiovascular causes, most of these deaths are in people over the age of 65. Of the five remaining deaths of the 1000 at least two will be due to cancer and one to two from various types of accident. What we have shown is that, in general, death rates in modern west-

TABLE 10:1

MORTALITY IN THE U.S. 1968

Cause	Number of deaths	Percent of total
Vascular diseases		
Heart disease	674,747	35
Cerebral vascular diseases	211,390	11
Other	154,155	8
Total	1,040,292	54
All forms of cancer	318,547	17
Accidents and violence		
Automobile accidents	54,862	3
Other accidents	64,317	3
Suicide	21,372	1
Homicide	14,686	1
Total	155,237	8
Respiratory diseases	123,440	6
Infant mortality	43,840	2
Congenital abnormalities	16,793	1
Infectious diseases	17,776	1
Total	1,715,925	89
All causes	1,930,082	100

Source: U.S. Department of Health, Education, and Welfare. *Vital Statistics of the United States.* Volume II. *Mortality.* Washington, D.C.: U.S. Government Printing Office, 1972.

Source: Cairns, J. (1978) Cancer, Science and Society W. H. Freeman and Company, San Francisco.

ern societies are low, and that most of the people who die are over the age of 65. A more detailed account of mortality is shown in Table 10:1.

If we look at deaths from a different point of view, in terms of years of working life lost, we find that the situation is somewhat different (Table 10:2). Twenty-six per cent of the working years lost are due to various types of accident and violence. Vascular diseases only account for 19 per cent of the working years lost, because most people dying from cardiovascular diseases are elderly. Infant mortality accounts for 14 per cent of the working years lost, and cancer makes up 13 per

TABLE 10:2

LOSS OF WORKING LIFESPAN IN THE U.S. 1968
FROM VARIOUS CAUSES

Cause	Work years lost*	Percent of total
Accidents and violence		
Automobile accidents	1,533,102	11
Other accidents	1,262,415	9
Homicide	397,668	3
Suicide	389,733	3
Total	3,582,918	26
Vascular diseases		
Heart disease	1,610,142	12
Cerebral vascular diseases	431,973	3
Other	578,801	4
Total	2,620,916	19
Infant mortality	1,970,489	14
Cancer	1,744,189	13
Respiratory diseases	968,064	7
Congenital diseases	674,465	5
Infectious diseases	291,185	2
Total	11,852,226	86
All causes	13,687,716	100

*Working life is considered to extend for 45 years, from age 20 to age 65. Deaths occurring before the age of 20 each contribute 45 lost years to the total, and those occurring between 20 and 65 contribute appropriately fewer, and deaths after 65 do not count.
Source: Cairns, J. (1978) Cancer, Science and Society. W. H. Freeman and Company, San Francisco.

cent. In other words, the serious *economic* effects of deaths are those deaths due to accidents and violence, cardiovascular diseases, infant mortality, and cancer. This is a somewhat different picture from that provided by the death data.

Another way of looking at the state of death of communities is to look at life tables. Life tables give us some idea of the expectation of life at various ages. In the United States in 1900–1902, the total expectation of life at birth—male and female, all races combined—was 49.24 years. That means that at that time, 80 years ago, an infant could expect to live for about 50 years. Compared with the average expectation in the Third World today, 50 years is a rather good figure. However, in the U.S. at present, the combined expectation of life, all races, male and female, is 73.2 years, a result of medical advances, improvement in the health of the community, and reduction in infant mortality. Currently men and women of age 65 can expect to live 16.3 years more. If we break down this statistic further, we find that white males can expect to live 13.9 years more and white females 18.4 years more.

What we conclude from these figures is that the population of North America and the western world is remarkably healthy in terms of survival figures. In spite of this, of course, people die. And it is not strange that 50 per cent of deaths are ascribed to cardiovascular causes; most of the victims are old, and at some point peoples' hearts must stop.

The Male Epidemic

During the same period of time, particularly since 1920, while there has been an overall increase in life expectation, there has also been an epidemic of ischemic heart disease, particularly in men. This is very well described by Dr. Terrence W. Anderson, who is now the Head of the Department of Preventive Medicine, University of British Columbia. His feeling is that atherosclerosis has remained more or less constant during this time, but that ischemic heart disease has increased. The reasons for this are still certainly not known. Diet may be a factor, but there are probably others. For example, the period between 1920 and 1980 saw a marked increase in cigaret smoking. Furthermore, people have generally grown more obese, and their jobs have become less physically demanding. There has been a vast increase in the use of machines, a vast increase in the use of oil, and considerable decrease in physical exertion. All these things, as far as we can tell, have some relationship to ischemic heart disease.

It is usual to assume that ischemic heart disease or coronary thrombosis is due to clots in the arteries, but this may not necessarily be true in all cases. In fact, the disease may be due to some change in the heart muscle itself. General nutrition might be behind it, or it might be due to particular foodstuffs. It might be due to stress or tobacco, or it might be due to certain imbalances, which we will discuss a little later. It may even be due to unsaturated fatty acids, which may cause focal degeneration of heart muscle in male animals. It has been shown that both unsaturated rapeseed oil and corn oil are toxic to the myocardium—in male test animals only. They do not affect female animals. Whether this bears any relationship with what happens in humans we do not know, but it is a surprising finding.

In the United States between 1909 and 1974, while the total fat intake has increased, the proportion of unsaturated fat in the diet has also increased. There has not been much change in the intake of cholesterol. Polyunsaturated fat intake has doubled between 1900 and 1974. During the same period, there has been a considerable increase in coronary heart disease. On the other hand, from an interesting paper from the Department of Community Health and Preventive Medicine, University Medical School, Chicago, it is clear that there was a considerable decline in coronary heart disease or ischemic heart disease in the United States during the period 1968 to 1975. Something has happened to people to change their response to their environment. The decline in coronary heart disease since 1968 may be related to the downturn in deaths from influenza and pneumonia, since we know that respiratory infection is often a complicating factor in cardiovascular deaths. What may also be partially responsible, and this cannot be proven, is that there is probably a decrease in cigaret smoking in certain adult men and women. It may also be that there is a decline in the consumption of saturated fat and cholesterol, and that some of this decline in death rates is due to the better detection, treatment, and control of hypertension. Certainly a decline in the number of fatal strokes is a direct result of this loss factor. These explanations are tentative but they are most interesting.

What we seem to have witnessed is that, since 1920, people have partially adapted to a new environment, one created by an industrialized society. This new environment includes better food, more calories, more fat, more alcohol, more cigarets, and less physical exertion.

Recently Dr. Robert E. Olson of the St. Louis University School of Medicine has made a splendid statement to the House Agriculture Committee concerning diet and heart disease. As he shows in Table 10:3, there has been a fall in death rates from coronary heart disease in certain countries, including the United States and Canada, between 1969 and 1973, while there has been an increase elsewhere, particularly in Scotland,

TABLE 10:3

TREND IN THE DEATH RATE FOR CORONARY HEART DISEASE SELECTED COUNTRIES, 1969–73 MALES AGE 45–54 YEARS

Country	Difference in Death Rate	Rate per 100,000 Population	
		1969	1973
United States	− 28.3	341.2	312.9
Canada	− 24.6	273.1	248.5
Australia	− 18.4	314.7	296.3
Finland	− 17.1	427.3	410.2
Israel	− 15.1	203.2	188.1
Japan	− 3.7	34.4	30.7
Austria	− 0.4	146.7	146.3
Italy	+ 0.6	112.9	113.5
Netherlands	+ 2.5	188.8	191.3
Switzerland	+ 4.1	103.4	107.5
Germany, F.R.	+ 9.3	146.4	155.7
Hungary	+ 21.5	142.8	164.3
Sweden	+ 30.1	126.0	156.1
Norway	+ 31.1	191.5	222.6
England and Wales	+ 31.6	254.9	286.5
Denmark	+ 31.9	159.5	191.4
Northern Ireland	+ 43.2	318.9	362.1
Scotland	+ 43.5	329.2	372.7

Source: Olson, R. E. (1980) Statement To the House Agriculture Subcommittee on Domestic Marketing, Consumer Relations and Nutrition, Nutrition Today 15:12–19.

England, and Denmark. These results are disturbing, and we have no explanation for them.

He concludes that atherosclerosis is a disease of unknown etiology and that the "Lipid-Hypothesis"—laying the blame at the door of saturated fats—is not proved and that it has failed as the basis for a strategy for the reduction of coronary heart disease.

A New Theory About Atherosclerosis

It would appear that there is something in modern life that is increasing the incidence of atherosclerosis, an arterial disease related to heart attacks and strokes. Plaque deposited on the walls of the arteries narrows the arterial passages and may start the formation of a blood clot, which may in turn shut down a critical artery in the heart, the brain, or other parts of the body. Of the many recent theories that have been advanced about atherosclerosis, perhaps the most interesting has come from Dr. Earl P. Benditt from the Department of Pathology, University of Washington School of Medicine, Seattle. His fascinating theory brings together aspects of biochemistry and cancer. He points out that the typical lesions of atherosclerosis as seen in autopsy are discrete lumps, elevations above the affected parts of the inside of artery that range in color from pearly gray to yellowish gray. Fatty substances from the blood serum in the artery wall give rise to deposits of cholesterol, which act as an irritant, causing inflammation and proliferation of cells. This theory, associated with a German pathologist, Rudolph Virchow, is supported by the increased rate of coronary heart disease among people with higher than normal levels of cholesterol in their blood.

Experimental work, particularly on chickens, has resulted in the view that the muscle cells in the arterial lesion become altered by mutation. There is also evidence that some cells in the lesion come from one single cell. Now it gets complicated. A specific enzyme—aryl hydrocarbon hydroxylase—produced in the liver converts certain substances—benzpyrene and methylcholanthrene—into mutagens capable of effecting the cellular change in the artery walls. These substances are present in low and very low density lipoproteins, of which cholesterol is one. Furthermore, the more lipoproteins present in the blood, the more of the enzyme is produced, producing in turn ever more mutagens.

It has also been established that blood lipoproteins are particularly good nutrients for culturing smooth muscle cells from the human artery wall. So that the artery wall cells are capable of converting into mutagens the pre-mutagenic substances that are transported to the cell by lipoproteins in the blood.

The intriguing aspect of this complex hypothesis is that it fits together all the factors that seem to be related to atherosclerosis: Dietary habits, cigaret smoking, changes in blood lipids, and hypertension. Heredity also plays a role in the level of blood lipoproteins. Certain families develop heart attacks more easily than others.

Benditt has also found that there seems to be a relationship between high blood pressure and cancer. People with hypertension have cells that are more susceptible to breakage by mutagens than people with normal blood pressure, and in fact there is evidence that the incidence of cancer is higher in people with hypertension. It is therefore suggested that there are subsets of human populations with an increased propensity for mutation in particular tissues such as the artery wall. This fascinating theory has been tested out in many laboratories. There is a connection between at least one dietary factor and cancer as well as atherosclerosis. Breast cancer rates have been found to be closely correlated world-wide by dietary fat intake, a correlation not unlike that found in deaths from heart disease. This is not proven, but it is at least an interesting hypothesis.

While ischemic heart disease may be mainly due to atherosclerosis, something else may also be influencing the heart muscle. In people who develop heart attacks, perhaps the heart muscle may also be influenced by mutagens or pre-mutagens, thus changing it and making it more susceptible to a lack of oxygen. The muscle may also be influenced by trace minerals such as magnesium and calcium.

Types of Heart Disease

The commonest cause in North America of heart disease is ischemic heart disease or coronary heart disease, a disease of the arteries leading to the heart that impairs the blood supply to the heart muscle. The term "ischemic heart disease" has been used synonomously with coronary heart disease to indicate that the manifestations are actually due to lack of blood flow to the heart rather than to the anatomic lesion in the coronary arteries as such. The condition is the result of, finally, a lack of oxygen to the heart muscle. Probably the commonest cause of coronary heart disease is atherosclerosis of the coronary arteries. We have mentioned that there are different opinions on this, and that most people feel that coronary heart disease is a result of a blockage of the coronary blood vessels, but there are some who believe that the coronary defect is a conduction defect within the heart muscle itself. There are other causes of ischemic heart disease, such as syphilitic disease of the aorta, which may interfere with coronary circulation, but this is relatively uncommon.

An early sign of impending coronary heart disease is angina pectoris, severe pain in the chest, the consequence of diminished blood supply to the heart muscle. Also often associated with ischemic heart disease is arterial hypertension or high blood pressure. About two thirds of all cases of high blood pressure are essential or idiopathic hypertension—this means that we do not know the cause. In some instances, though, the cause is found, the commonest being kidney disease. Another cause, relatively uncommon, is a tumor pheochromocytoma, in which too much adrenaline (epinephrine) is produced. Associated with and related to ischemic heart disease are defects in the condition of electrical impulses in the heart. These diagnoses are made by a physician, usually with the aid of an electrocardiograph.

A disease of the heart which used to be more common in North America and western Europe is mitral stenosis, a deformity and narrowing of the mitral valve in the left side of the heart, usually the consequence of rheumatic fever. In rheumatic fever the valve leaflets are scarred and deformed. In North America this type of disease is usually confined to older people, developed at a time when rheumatic fever was more common than it is now. Another form of heart disease is aortic stenosis, in which there is a narrowing of the aorta. This may be due to rheumatic fever, or it may be a congenital defect. It is interesting that rheumatic fever is now common in the Third World countries, that is, tropical countries, particularly those in Africa, probably because of widespread overcrowding, malnutrition, and general susceptibility to infection, situations that used to be common in North America and western Europe 30 years ago.

What also must be considered in connection with heart disease is that congenital defects in the cardiovascular system occur in about one out of every 100 births, although the cause can be determined in only about 3 per cent of cases. German measles (rubella) early in pregnancy may damage the fetal heart as well as other organs. Impaired blood flow is a common manifestation of a defect, which may be the narrowing of a heart valve or constriction of the aorta. Another defect is a left-to-right shunt, in which some oxygenated blood moves from the left to the right side of the heart instead of emptying entirely into the arterial system. The cause may be a hole in the wall between the auricles of the heart or between the two ventricles, or there may be other defects such as a communication or tube between the aorta and the pulmonary artery (patent ductus arteriosus). Fortunately, congenital heart disease in most cases can be effectively treated by modern surgery.

Diet and Coronary Heart Disease

More than 60 years ago Professor Anitschkow produced apparent atherosclerosis in animals by feeding them high-cholesterol diets. This was at about the time that the great epidemic of human ischemic heart disease started. While we have collected a great deal of information since that time, the causes of the disease are by no means clear. In monkeys, diets rich in cholesterol and saturated fat do produce high serum cholesterols and aortic and coronary atherosclerosis. Furthermore, in animals a cholesterol-free diet has produced a regression in atherosclerosis, and there is evidence that this is also possible in humans.

From experiment it is clear that there is some relationship between dietary cholesterol, plasma cholesterol levels, and the development and regression of experimental atherosclerosis. However, in humans the relationships between cholesterol intake and serum cholesterol are not quite direct. It would seem that dietary cholesterol has a decisive effect upon plasma cholesterol concentration from approximately zero cholesterol per day to 300 to 600 mg per day. In this range there is a consistent increase in serum cholesterol, but above this, a further increase in cholesterol intake over 500 to 600 mg per day does not usually substantially increase serum cholesterol concentrations. This means that, when people are already on a high cholesterol diet, the addition of an extra egg or two per day will not make much difference to the total plasma cholesterol. There is controversy about saturated and polyunsaturated fats. In recent work, Dr. E. H. Ahrens and colleagues show that increments in saturated fatty acids in the diet increase serum cholesterol levels, while polyunsaturated fatty acids tend to diminish them.

We know that vegetarians and people who live on non-western diets have lower rates of ischemic heart disease than the average in United States or Canada. It should also be realized that among Seventh-Day Adventists, who do not smoke, drink tea or coffee, or indulge in a high alcohol intake; the disease rate is low. In general, however, it can be said that people on vegetarian diets or diets with a low intake of animal foods have less atherosclerosis than people in our society.

In large population groups, when very different dietary patterns are studied, there does seem to be a relationship between levels of saturated fat and cholesterol consumption and the serum cholesterol levels. However, if culturally homogeneous groups are studied, we experience difficulty in finding a significant correlation between nutrient intakes, blood lipids, and coronary heart disease. In general one would advise a decrease in fat intake and an increase in unsaturated fats, but this type of advice is not generally accepted by all cardiologists. It is difficult with homogeneous populations to find significant correlations between dietary data and clinical cardiovascular measurements because of limitations of methodology. Appropriate diets can reduce serum cholesterol levels and, if this is accompanied by weight reduction, the results are in the direction of lower serum cholesterol. However, clinical trials have not yet proven that this type of manipulation will be advantageous. It is also interesting that there may be some evidence that vegetable protein, such as soybean protein, may reduce the serum cholesterol. If this is accompanied by a low cholesterol and a low saturated fat intake the results may even be more favorable.

From the National Co-operative Pooling Project of the American Heart Association it is quite clear that there is doubling of cardiovascular disease for people with serum cholesterols above 250-mg per 100 mℓ, and this rate triples when serum cholesterol goes above 300 mg per 100 mℓ of blood. About one third of North Americans have plasma cholesterol levels above 250 mg per 100 mℓ of blood. Most of them appear to have a genetic predisposition that brings this about; the condition is brought about partially by their diet, but it is not merely a question of diet. It may also be related to other factors—lack of exercise, obesity, and cigaret smoking. There is still a matter of controversy whether the modest reduction in fat or saturated fat intake will produce any great effect on coronary heart disease. Since 1970 the American diet has been changing in the direction of a decreased intake of dietary cholesterol and in the amount of polyunsaturated fats ingested. There has also been a reduction in milk and cream, butter, and egg consumption. Death rates from ischemic heart disease have also declined during the last 12 years, but whether this reduction in death rate can be ascribed only to dietary changes is impossible to determine, because at the same time there has been some increase in jogging and exercise, and at least in certain groups there has been a reduction in cigaret smoking.

Some Dissenting Voices

It is very easy to have a simplistic approach to this question of ischemic heart disease and atherosclerosis. The simplistic approach is that, if we reduce total fat and if we increase polyunsaturated fats, miraculously heart disease and atherosclerosis will disappear. This is not true. The evidence we have already examined indicates that in general, if we study populations all over the world, there is less atherosclerosis in communities that have a low fat intake. There is also less or no ischemic heart disease in communities on diets that contain not only low fat, but low protein and a high proportion of natural, unrefined carbohydrates. We must also remember that in these communities where there is very little ischemic heart disease, there have also been periods of starvation and a great deal of very hard physical exercise. And many of these people die young. All these matters are intimately involved in the question of atherosclerosis. If we look at matters quite coldly we do not know with accuracy the causes of atherosclerosis. We have many suggestions but no good evidence.

11.

Hypoglycemia, Hyperactivity, and Food Allergy

Close to the building where I work, the following plaque has been erected:

The Discovery of Insulin 1921. At a meeting of the University of Toronto Physiological Journal Club held on November 14th, 1921, in a building which stood on this site, Frederick Banting, an orthopedic surgeon, and Charles H. Best, a recent graduate in Physiology and Biochemistry, made the first public announcement of their discovery of a therapy for use in the treatment of diabetes mellitus. On January 11th, 1922, Insulin, originally called Isletin, was administered to 14-year old Leonard Thompson, at the Toronto General Hospital. The dramatic improvement of the patient and widespread publicity during the next 6 months brought the scientists universal acclaim. The discovery, a combination of 9 months of intensive effort, has prolonged the lives of millions of diabetics throughout the world.

Hypoglycemia

Diabetes is in some ways the opposite of hypoglycemia. Hypoglycemia is an abnormally low blood sugar level, while one of the many manifestations of diabetes mellitus is a high blood sugar level. Study of both these aspects of blood chemistry was greatly stimulated by the work of Banting and Best.

Hypoglycemia is a problem associated with a number of diseases. One is a tumor of the cells in the pancreas that make insulin. Various type of liver damage are another, or it may be due to deficiency in the cortex of the adrenal gland, resulting from infections, tumors, or hemorrhage into the glands. Hypoglycemia may also be found in hypopituitarism, and certain malignant growths may be associated with severe hypoglycemia. It has recently been found that certain people with mild diabetes may have spontaneous episodes of hypoglycemia occurring about three hours after meals in the early phases of the disease. In other words, some people complaining of low blood sugar may be in the early phases of the development of diabetes mellitus.

All of these are serious diseases. Obviously, then, if a person suspects that he or she is suffering from hypoglycemia, an expert internist or endocrinologist should be consulted to determine the exact causes. This is not an area for self-diagnosis or consultation with a health-food dealer.

Particularly in the United States, it has been fashionable in recent years for various people, many of them completely unqualified in medicine, to pontificate on the subject of hypoglycemia. In fact, a cult has developed in connection with hypoglycemia in the United States.

Temporary or functional hypoglycemia—that is, not associated with serious disease—may be the consequence of oversecretion of insulin by islet cells of the pancreas following on an excessive response to high sugar consumption. It may also be found after severe muscular exertion, and also in generally poor nutrition during pregnancy and lactation. On examination, many such patients do not have too much insulin in the blood, so there are unknown factors that modify the response of the liver and the tissues to insulin. We do not know all the reasons for this type of hypoglycemia.

Symptoms of Hypoglycemia

Hypoglycemia attacks tend to occur several hours after meals when the person is hungry. They are frequently noticeable after someone has previously eaten a great deal of sugar. The first symptoms include sweating, flushing or numbness, a feeling of cold, hunger, trembling, headaches, dizziness, weakness, elevated pulse rate, palpitations, increased blood pressure, onsets of fear, and sometimes fainting. These are similar to the symptoms of diabetics who have received too much insulin. If the condition is not relieved by taking sugar or glucose, there are signs of the involvement of the central nervous system, including restlessness, thick speech, emotional instability, and other symptoms. The victim is also unco-ordinated; hand and foot movements are not balanced, and he or she may see double. In extreme cases, convulsions follow, and in very few cases there may be coma and death.

Differential Diagnosis

The differential diagnosis of hypoglycemia is important, and it must be done by a skilled physician. Some of the symptoms described are sometimes seen in anxiety states or in certain epinephrine-producing tumors. The convulsive and comatose stages of hypoglycemia call for a careful differential diagnosis, which may include epilepsy, brain tumor, uremia, and eclampsia. And in diabetic patients a distinction must be made between, insulin shock and diabetic coma. Simple hypoglycemia is that associated with severe muscular exertion and/or general poor nutrition, or with individuals who normally secrete too much insulin—often obese people. In ordinary simple hypoglycemia, the treatment is by giving glucose promptly if the patient can swallow, 10 to 20 g of glucose, or a supplement of sugar or candy or orange juice or honey.

Diet for Hypoglycemia

Ordinary hypoglycemia, not related to serious illness, can be treated by dietary measures—frequent small meals high in protein and fat, low in carbohydrate, including a snack on waking and another on retiring. For adults a satisfactory diet should be composed of 120 to 140 g of protein and 80 to 100 g of carbohydrates with a reasonable amount of fat. People who suffer hypoglycemic attacks should always carry sugar or other rapidly available carbohydrate with them. On the other hand, they will experience fewer attacks if they stay away from large amounts of sugar in their diet. It should also be remembered that hypoglycemia may be induced by alcohol; whether chronic low blood sugar may contribute to alcoholism is another matter that has not been settled.

The hypoglycemic's diet should include lean meat, poultry, and fish cooked in any way preferred. Fish should be eaten frequently. Other good sources of protein are cottage cheese as well as other types of cheese. Seasonal vegetables should be included—kale, cauliflower, green beans, eggplant, asparagus, lettuce, tomato, cucumber, and spinach. Preferred fruits are the ones lowest in carbohydrates—berries, melons, peaches, pears, apples, oranges, and grapefruit. Obviously candied fruits should be avoided. Beverages should be weak tea, water, decaffeinated coffee, skim milk, prune juice. Alcohol or strong coffee or tea, particularly with a great deal of sugar added, are best avoided. Starchy foods should be avoided, as should prepared foods bought in supermarkets—cakes, pies, cookies, chewing gum, gravies, and so on. Many dressings and ketchup contain a great deal of sugar. As a matter of fact, it is very difficult to purchase foods that don't contain sugar. Candies and chocolate are out, as are sugar-containing drinks.

It's a good idea to start the day, immediately on getting up in the morning, with a milkshake made with milk and some added milk powder, flavored if desired. Breakfast should include high-protein foods—ham or bacon, two eggs, or cheese, fish, or other forms of meat. At about 11:00 o'clock a snack is in order—perhaps some cheese or skimmed milk. For lunch, fish or poultry, lean meat or frankfurters, or sardines, tuna, salmon, and a high-protein mid-afternoon snack. At the evening meal there should be some fruit juice or skimmed milk or lean meat as required, and before retiring a snack of fruit or protein from animal sources is recommended. It may be possible to change over completely to a diet containing a great deal of protein from plant sources and whole grain, but most people in North America would find this a little difficult. If a carbohydrate is used, it should preferably be from whole grain sources.

Obese people who suffer from hypoglycemia are another problem, but they can be dealt with by sensible nutritional management.

Hyperactive Children

The term "hyperactive" does not apply to one particular disease or condition. It is a general catch-all description of certain children. Hyperactive children are excitable, fidgety, can't keep still; they touch everything and everyone in the vicinity. They are easily distracted—unable to concentrate because of a short attention span. They jump from one activity to the other. In addition they are impulsive, irritable, unpredictable; they are quick-tempered, explosive, and they panic easily. If they suffer from hypoglycemia, as some do, the bad temper increases. They have a low tolerance for frustration and failure, and they demand immediate gratification of needs. They often have some learning disabilities; in general their school performance is not commensurate with their intelligence quotient. Sometimes they suffer from dyslexia, an impaired ability to learn to read. In addition, they may be aggressive and have difficulties with their peers and adults. At other times they may be depressed and suffer from low self-esteem.

Sometimes the term "hyperactive" has been used synonymously with "minimal brain dysfunction" (MBD). This is not correct, as it suggests that there is a disorder of the brain responsible for the hyperactive syndrome. While it may be that some hyperactive children show some signs associated with minimal brain dysfunction, many do not. And, on the other hand, some children with minimal brain dysfunction do not always show the cardinal features of the hyperactivity syndrome.

We should remember that hyperactivity characterizes a heterogenous group of children suffering from a number of different conditions. Hyperactivity has been found in association with hyperthyroidism, which is an overactivity of the thyroid gland; in hypoglycemia, lead poisoning, certain allergic conditions, sometimes in deafness or blindness, and sometimes in the diseases of the central nervous system following on acute encephalitis and other conditions. It may also occur in children with emotional disorders, with personality disorders, with depression, and those suffering from psychoses. It may well be that certain causes of hyperactivity may be involved in metabolic disturbances of the brain, many of which are currently being investigated, and in abnormalities of the physiology of the nervous system. We should make it quite clear that the diagnosis of hyperactivity is a complex task. It should be a co-operative effort of teachers, parents, psychologists, and physicians. And among the physicians, those best qualified to diagnose hyperactivity are internists, neurologists, and psychiatrists who have a special interest in children and their problems.

We do have the impression that the number of hyperactive children has increased during recent years. Of course, the measurement depends on the diagnostic criteria used and the population studied. In the United States and in the Netherlands, a prevalence of 5 to 20 per cent has been reported in school-age children. In Britain, few children are found who are classified as hyperactive. In California it has been said that 40 per cent of an entire elementary school population suffers from hyperactivity. We take this statement with a pinch of salt. Other people suggest that about 5 per cent of the elementary school population are "hyperactive." We must be careful here about what constitutes hyperactivity. Normal, active, inquisitive, lively children are not "hyperactive." They are normal children, and it takes some skill to distinguish between "normal" and "abnormal" in this area.

The Good Parent and the Good Teacher

Good teachers and caring parents may be able to induce hyperactive children to become more stable and to grow up into good citizens. We should remember that a very hyperactive child, Winston Churchill, who was born in 1876, became a rather successful citizen; he was loved and cherished by his nanny. Another hyperactive child was Thomas A. Edison. He could not be educated at school and was taught at home by his remarkable mother.

It must be very difficult for active little boys and girls to sit still in school. And if they are unhappy at home, they may develop apparent hyperactivity in order to get affection and attention. At least half of hyperactivity cases seen in school children are identified in the classroom. A hundred years ago many children did not go to school, so they could be hyperactive without anyone's noticing. At that time children who did not make it at school worked. Boys became miners or ditchdiggers, cowboys or mule skinners, loggers or pickers of cotton and corn. Girls cooked and sewed and cleaned. These jobs didn't require book learning, and it might well be that many children are not really designed for book learning in the type of constricted society into which we are now forcing them.

We know that there are more hyperactive boys than girls, and that this excess number cannot be ascribed to prenatal or birth injuries, to salicylates, or to food additives. In our modern society there aren't many things boys can do to work off excess energy. There are no cows to be milked. There are no sheep to be shorn and there are no fields through which they can wander. In a society where sitting in front of television sets is the premier pastime, there is little opportunity for small boys and girls to take the exercise they need.

Physical and Chemical Causes of Hyperactivity

In most cases no cause can be found for hyperactivity, but no treatment can be prescribed until we have tried to find the cause. One of the best books on the subject is *Help for the Hyperactive Child* by Dr. Sydney Walker, III, of the Southern California Neuropsychiatric Institute. The first part of the examination of the hyperactive child is a very detailed and comprehensive medical examination accompanied by whatever chemical or other tests may be necessary. We must very carefully rule out physical causes before we decide to treat a child with a particular drug.

Among Dr. Walker's case histories there are a number of interesting physical causes of hyperactivity. One child who was diagnosed as hyperactive was suffering from pinworms. She was sleepless, tired, and fidgety. When the worms were treated, her condition improved. Obviously all cases are not that simple. In another small girl most of the neurological findings were normal; however, it was found that the optic arteries had crystallized deposits along the perimeters, and there seemed to be enlarged blood vessels in the retina. The final diagnosis was that of a congenital heart condition that prevented a normal flow of oxygenated blood to the brain. When the heart condition was corrected, the child was no longer hyperactive.

Another cause of hyperactivity is serious head or neck injury occurring in early childhood. These are becoming more common in a mechanized society, and they should be considered in the diagnosis of hyperactivity. Of course, the treatment of such injuries is extremely difficult, as there may be brain damage involved.

There is no doubt that, in an increasingly chemical world, substances in the environment or in the food may in certain circumstances be responsible for hyperactivity in children. It is a long and tedious business to discover which of these may be responsible. Lead poisoning is one element that may produce hyperactivity. Other chemical poisons to which children have access are glue and gasoline, both of which are often deliberately inhaled, and hard drugs. In some settings, mercury poisoning should be considered. A final possibility is depression, which is a diagnosis to be made by a psychiatrist.

Drugs and Hyperactivity

For some years now hyperactive children have been treated with drugs, mainly Ritalin and Dexedrine, both belonging to the amphetamine group. In some cases treatment is successful, but often it is not. These drugs are sometimes given indiscriminantly for long periods of time without adequate medical supervision, and the risks in such treatment are considerable. In the first place, these drugs are appetitite suppressants—young children who take them may not grow properly. Furthermore, children may become addicted to these drugs. There are also side effects, which may include nervousness and insomnia, skin rashes, dizziness, palpitation, headaches, drowsiness, changes in blood pressure, rapid or irregular heartbeat.

One of the other drugs given to hyperactive children is Tofranil. This drug can produce difficulty in focusing the eyes and it may produce glaucoma, as well as other serious symptoms.

The prolonged use of some amphetamines has produced psychoses similar to paranoid schizophrenia that has been associated with homicide. Some children on these drugs may develop hallucinations. One described his experience as seeing a row of colors, lions, tigers, and elephants marching around in a whirlpool of lights. These are extreme reactions, but they should be considered by physicians and parents before they give children these drugs. The whole question of drug treatment of hyperactivity is controversial and, while drugs are useful, they should only be given under skilled and meticulous medical supervision. There is a considerable danger that children on drugs become part of the general drug culture.

Food Additives and Hyperactivity

We have already touched on the claims of Dr. Ben Feingold that food additives are responsible for a great number of cases of hyperactivity. Drs. Morris A. Lipton, Charles B. Nemeroff, and Richard B. Mailman of the University of North Carolina School of Medicine have done further work on Dr. Feingold's hypothesis and have concluded that about 25 per cent of hyperactive children are reported to show diminution of many of their symptoms at school when on the Feingold additive-free diet. While Dr. Feingold's claims are not completely substantiated by subsequent clinical trials, he has raised an issue of considerable importance: In individual children certain chemical substances, which may be food additives, may have a deleterious effect.

However, parents should not try the Feingold diet until the child has been carefully tested by a skilled physician to exclude other possible physical causes. For instance, one of the cases of hyperactivity mentioned by Dr. Sydney Walker was a child suffering from carbon monoxide poisoning from the school bus. When he was taken out of the school bus, his hyperactive behavior stopped. Another fascinating case quoted by Dr. Walker was that of a small girl who received large multiple vitamin supplements, which included vitamins B, A, D and E. On careful chemical testing excessively high concentrations of vitamin A were found in her blood. When the large doses of vitamin A and other vitamins were discontinued, the child became normal, but it took a number of years to undo the effects of the multiple vitamin dosage.

Medical Diagnosis

In conclusion, we repeat that hyperactive children should be carefully treated and medically diagnosed. There are no cure-alls for all the conditions classified under the term "hyperactivity." There is no universal drug, no universal diet, that will cure it. Every child must be considered individually, using all skills that are available.

Food Allergy

Hyperactivity and allergic conditions are quite often associated. There are even some suggestions that *all* hyperactivity is rooted in allergic states. Some people also think that it is part of an allergy-tension-fatigue (ATF) syndrome.

Allergy or hypersensitivity is a condition in which the body has developed an altered reaction to foreign material. This reaction produces some tissue injury, which is the allergic reaction. In the human body if there is a bacterial intruder or a virus intruder, such as the measles virus, this antigen is met by defender antibodies in the bloodstream and the capillaries. Allergy is an expression of an immunological response in the body. The invading substances are termed allergens, and the defending antibodies are called reagins. The allergen invaders are usually less threatening than the viruses and microbes that can cause major infectious diseases. Allergens do not produce lifelong immunity like an attack of measles. The reagins can cause damage to the body tissues that they are trying to protect. In relatively mild cases of allergy, hives, asthma, and hay fever can result from excessive activity of the reagins. There may be serious consequences when hypersensitivity exists to drugs, chemicals, and some infectious micro-organisms. For instance when someone has become sensitized to a drug such as penicillin, his reaction may be very serious when he is given this allergen again.

The so-called allergy-tension-fatigue syndrome is manifested by someone who has an "allergic-looking" face—wrinkles around the eyes, black circles under the eyes, puffiness below or on the side of the eyes, and wrinkles on the nose. The patient is pale, dull, and apathetic. (It is interesting that this appearance is similar to the "amphetamine" look produced by amphetamines and amphetamine-like drugs.) It has been stated that the ATF syndrome should be diagnosed on the basis of patient and family history of allergy, and by feeding problems and hyperactive behavior in infancy, including listlessness, marked perspiration, and strong cravings for certain foods, such as peanuts, chocolate, and milk.

We must not, however, fall into the trap of ascribing all these symptoms to a single cause. There is no doubt that headache can be produced by allergic response to chocolate, to licorice, or to monosodium glutamate. But it may also be caused by eyestrain, tension, or diseases. So the diagnosis of an allergic state or an allergic reaction should be made by an allergist, not by the parents of the child or their well-meaning friends.

Food allergies are common, and some people think that such allergies are a frequent cause of the many allergic manifestations in most tissues of the body. A person may be allergic to a single or several foods, and food allergy may occur and continue at any age.

Common Food Allergies

Allergic consequences may be found in many tissues of the body. In infancy, allergy to cow's milk is very often the cause of nasal-bronchial symptoms, colic, and other digestive symptoms. We also find dermatitis and eczema and unusual restlessness, irritability, and discomfort, particularly when homogenized cow's milk is given as a supplement to breast milk. Allergy to eggs is also common in infancy.

Allergies in young adults may be the partial cause of asthma, chronic bronchitis, and broncho-spasm. They may also be involved in headaches, eczema, and a long list of other conditions: Fever, recurrent colds, post-nasal mucus, dermatitis, contact dermatitis, and a number of gastrointestinal allergic responses such as vomiting, regional ileitis, and irritable bowel. Food allergy may also produce migraine, sick headaches, arthritis of special types, and eye problems, including inflammation of the eyelids and ocular pains. It may also be involved in dermatitis of the ear and ear canal. It may produce allergic cystitis and bladder spasm. It has also been suggested that there may be an allergic element in cardiac irregularities or arrhythmias.

Elimination Diets

In order to discover to which food people are allergic, various elimination diets are used. A common one is the cereal-free diet worked out by Drs. Rowe, father and son, from Oakland, California. This diet contains tapioca, white potatoes, sweet potatoes, soybean potato bread, lima bean potato bread, soy milk, lamb, chicken, bacon, lamb liver, apricots, grapefruit, lemon, peaches, pineapples, prunes, pears, cane or beet sugar, salt, sesame oil, soybean oil, and gelatin. Only margarine made of hydrogenated soybean oil is used. Also included in the diet are peas, spinach, squash, green beans, artichokes, asparagus, carrots, lettuce, lima beans, white vinegar, vanilla extract, lemon extract, cornstarch-free baking powder, cream of tartar, and maple syrup, either natural or synthetic.

Excluded are all foods that may produce allergy. All cereal grains, including rice, rye, corn, and especially wheat are banned. All eggs, milk, and other dairy products, including butter, cheese, cream, and any food containing the slightest traces of milk, are excluded. Fish, pork, and a number of vegetables, especially those of the cabbage family, and many fruits, including oranges, apples, bananas, and melons, are excluded. The only oil allowed is soybean oil, and tea is allowed when we add it. It is interesting that chicken is allowed in the diet, but hens are not permitted. The reason for this is that the hens may have unlaid eggs which often are broken; a small amount of egg left on the carcass of the hen produces symptoms if eaten by a very sensitive individual.

Allergy diagnosis with the use of this basic diet is complex, although the premise is simple: As foods are added, one at a time, the allergic reaction is discovered. Such a program should only be carried out under the direction of a skilled physician or nutritionist. It is very important that the patient not lose weight and gets enough calcium, electrolytes, and vitamins.

12.

The Chemical Feast

It's a complex world we live in. Scientific and technological advances are progressing with mind-boggling speed, leaving many of us confused and apprehensive. The question of chemicals in our diet and in our environment and how they may be affecting us is an awesome one, and one that many people feel overwhelmed by. Most of us haven't the knowledge and expertise to form judgments about the risks involved, and ignorance foments fear.

The purpose of this book was to dispel some of the worry by explaining some simple facts about chemicals in our total environment. One thing is clear: You don't have to be a highly trained chemist or clinician to exercise common sense. If there is a central theme uniting the disparate topics in this book, it is that we must maintain a sense of proportion in all things. Certainly we must continue to put pressure on government and industry to police the substances they are introducing into the environment. But at the same time, we must not give way to panic. We must remember that the amounts of these materials we are exposed to are extremely small. As we have pointed out, at present there are far greater risks in our lives than those inherent in our food, and there are far more serious dangers in bacterial and viral food poisoning than there are in chemical additives, intentional or incidental.

One final, if sobering, point: Death comes to us all. Barring accidents and violence, most of us will die of a disease. As the body ages, we simply cannot prevent some form of disease from finally overcoming it. The best we can do is to use our common sense and the best advice of trained and knowledgable people to evolve a life style most conducive to the longest, healthiest possible life.

Selected References

Chemicals and the Normal Diet

Borgstrom, G. (1968). *Principles of Food Science,* two volumes. Macmillan Company, Collier-Macmillan Limited, London.

Burton, B. T. (1965). *The Heinz Handbook of Nutrition.* Blakiston Division, McGraw-Hill Book Company, New York.

Deutsch, R. M. (1971). *The Family Guide to Better Food and Better Health.* Creative Home Library, Meredith Corporation, Des Moines, Iowa.

Fleck, H. (1971). *Introduction to Nutrition,* Second Edition. Macmillan Company, Collier-Macmillan Ltd., London.

Goodhart, R. S., and Shils, M. E. (1973). *Modern Nutrition in Health and Disease,* Fifth Edition. Lea and Febiger, Philadelphia.

Hall, R. H. (1974). *Food for Nought.* Harper and Row, Publishers, Hagerstown, Maryland.

le Riche, W. H. (1980). *The Complete Family Book of Nutrition and Meal Planning.* Methuen Publications, Agincourt, Ontario.

Major, R. H. (1954). *A History of Medicine,* two volumes. Charles C. Thomas, Springfield, Illinois.

Singer, C., and Underwood, E. A. (1962). *A Short History of Medicine.* Oxford at the Clarendon Press, Oxford University Press.

Trager, T. (1970). *The Foodbook.* Grossman Publishers, New York.

Whitehead, R. G. (1979). "Dietary Goals: Their Scientific Justification." *Journal of the Royal Society of Health,* 5:181–184.

Dietary Changes and Malnutrition

Cooper, R., Stamler, J., Dyer, A., and Garside D. (1978). "The Decline in Mortality from Coronary Heart Disease. U.S.A. 1968–1975." *Journal of Chronic Disease*, 31:709–720.

Everson, G. J. (1960). "Bases for Concern About Teenagers' Diets." *Journal of the American Dietetic Association*, 36:17–21.

Gortner, W. A. (1975). "Nutrition in The United States, 1900 to 1974." *Cancer Research*, 35:3246–3253.

Hodges, R. E., and Krehl, W. A. "Nutritional Status of Teenagers in Iowa." *American Journal of Clinical Nutrition*, 17:200–210.

Lloyd, F. G., (1969). "Finally, Facts on Malnutrition in The United States." *Today's Health*, September, 32,33,80.

Nutrition Canada (1973). *Nutrition, A National Priority.* Department of National Health and Welfare, Ottawa.

Vital Statistics of the United States (1977). *Life Tables*, Volume II—Section 5. U.S. Department of Health, Education, and Welfare, Public Health Service National Center for Health Statistics, DHEW Publication No. (PHS) 80–1104, Hyattsville, Maryland 1980.

Food Additives and Illness

Bender, A. E. (1978). *Food Processing and Nutrition.* Academic Press, London, New York.

Borgstrom, G. (1968). *Principles of Food Science*, two volumes. The Macmillan Company, Collier-Macmillan Limited, London.

Boyd, E. M. (1973). *Toxicity of Pure Foods.* Chemical Rubber Company Press, Cleveland, Ohio.

Cordle, F., and Kolbye, A. C. (1979). "Food Safety and Public Health." *Cancer*, May Supplement, 43:2143–2150.

Frobish, R. A., and Van Houweling, C. D. (1978). "Symposium: Wise Use of Chemicals, Drugs and Additives by Dairy Producers." *Journal of Dairy Science*, 61:660–664.

Furia, T. E. (editor) (1968). *Handbook of Food Additives.* Chemical Rubber Company, Cleveland, Ohio.

Galli, C. L., Paoletti, R., and Vetlorazzi, G. (editors) (1978). *Chemical Toxicology of Food.* Proceedings of the International Symposium on Chemical Toxicology of Food. Milan. June 9–10, 1978. Elsevier/North-Holland Biomedical Press. Amsterdam.

Goodhart, R. S., and Shils, M. E. (1980). *Modern Nutrition in Health and Disease,* Sixth Edition. Lea and Febiger, Philadelphia.

Hall, R. H. (1974). *Food for Thought. The Decline in Nutrition.* Harper and Row, Publishers, Hagerstown, Maryland.

Irving, G. W. (1978). "Safety Evaluation of the Food Ingredients Called GRAS." *Nutrition Reviews,* 36:351–356.

Jackson, T. A. (editor) (1980). *Mercury Pollution in the Wabgon English River System of Northwestern Ontario and Possible Remedical Measures.* A Progress Report for 1978–1979. Prepared by the Steering Committee, Government of Canada, Government of Ontario. Publisher not stated.

Jenkins, C. L. (1978). "Textile Dyes are Potential Hazards." *Journal of Environmental Health,* 40:256–263.

Jukes, T. H. (1978). "How Safe is Our Good Supply?" *Archives of Internal Medicine,* 138:772–774.

Jukes, T. H. (1979). "Carcinogens in Food and The Delaney Clause." *Journal of the American Medical Association,* 241:617–619.

Khera, K. S. (1976). "Significance of Metabolic Patterns in Teratogenic Testing for Food Safety." *Clinical Toxicology,* 9:773–790.

le Riche, W. H. (1976). "Epidemiology in Food Safety Evaluation. Past and Present." *Clinical Toxicology,* 9(5):665–690.

Minister of National Health and Welfare, Canada (1980). *Food Additives: What Do You Think?* Report on Opinion Survey conducted Summer 1979. Minister of Supply and Services, Canada, Ottawa, Ontario.

Morley, H. B. (1978). "An Appeal for Reason." *Food Cosmetics and Toxicology,* 16:373–377.

News and Comment (1978). "Ever So Cautiously the FDA Moves Towards a Ban on Nitrites." *Science,* 201:887–889.

Oser, B. L. (1975). "Food Additives," pp. 299–305 from *Dangerous Properties of Industrial Materials,* Fourth Edition, edited by N. Irving Sax. Van Nostrand Reinhold Company, Toronto.

Oser, B. L. (1976). "Are Food Additives Overregulated?" Reprint from *Food Drug Cosmetic Law Journal,* pp. 627–635.

Oser, B. L. (1978). "Benefit/Risk: Whose? What? How Much?" *Food Technology,* August, pp. 55–58. Reprint.

Packard, V. S. (1976). *Processed Foods and The Consumer.* University of Minnesota Press, Minneapolis, Minnesota.

Palm, P. E., Arnold, E. P., Rachwall, P. C., Leyczer, J. C., Teague, K. W., and Kensler, C. J. (1978). "Evaluation of the Teratogenic Potential of Fresh-Brewed Coffee and Caffeine in the Rat." *Toxicology and Applied Pharmacology,* 44:1–16.

Riemann, H. (1969). *Food-Borne Infections and Intoxications.* Academic Press, New York and London.

Scott, P. P. (1979). "Food Additives and Contaminants." *The Practitioner,* 222:648–655.

Select Committee on Sugar Substitutes (1978). "Saccharin." *Diabetes,* 27:878–880.

Shubik, P. (1979). "Food Additives (Natural and Synthetic)." *Cancer,* 43:1982–1986.

Zimbelman, R. G. (1979). "Scientific Basis for Interpretation of Delaney Clause." *Journal of Animal Science,* 48:986–992.

Natural Poisons in Food

Andersson, K. E., and Johansson, M. (1973). "Effects of Viscotoxin on Rabbit Heart and Aorta, and on Frog Skeletal Muscle." *European Journal of Pharmacology,* 23:223–231.

Bannister, B., Ginsburg, R., and Sneerson, J. (1977). "Cardiac Arrest due to Liquorice-induced Hypokalaemia." *British Medical Journal.* 2:738–739.

Benner, M. H. and Lee, H. J. (1973). "Anaphylactic Reaction to Chamomile Tea." *Journal of Allergy and Clinical Immunology,* 52:307–308.

Berglund, F. (1978). "Food Additives." *Archives of Toxicology,* Supplement, 1:33–46.

Bryson, P. D. (1978). Letter To the Editor: "Burdock Root Tea Poisoning." *Journal of the American Medical Association,* 240:1586.

Chamberlain, T. J. (1970). Letter To The Editor: "Licorice Poisoning, Pseudoaldosteronism and Heart Failure." *Journal of the American Medical Association,* 213:1343.

Goodhart, R. S., and Shils, M. E. (editors) 1980). *Modern Nutrition in Health and Disease,* Sixth Edition. Lea and Febiger, Philadelphia.

Koster, M., and David, G. K. (1968). "Reversible Severe Hypertension Due To Licorice Ingestion." *New England Journal of Medicine,* 278:1381–1383.

Last, J. M., (1980) (editor) Maxcy-Rosenau. *Public Health and Preventive Medicine,* Eleventh Edition. Appleton-Century-Crofts, New York.

Lewis, W. H. (1978). Letter To the Editor: "Reporting Adverse Reactions to Herbal Ingestants." *Journal of the American Medical Association,* 240:109–110.

McGee, J. O'D., Patrick, R. S., Wood, C. B., and Blumgart, L. H. (1976). "A Case of Veno-occlusive Disease of the Liver in Britain Associated with Herbal Tea Consumption." *Journal of Clinical Pathology,* 29:788–794.

Napke, E. (1976). *Poison Control Statistics.* Health and Welfare Canada. Ottawa.

Riemann, H. (1969). *Food-Borne Infections and Intoxications.* Academic Press, New York, London.

Sayre, J. W., and Kaymakcalan, S. (1964). "Hazards To Health, Cyanide Poisoning from Apricot Seeds among Children in Central Turkey." *New England Journal of Medicine,* 270:1113–1115.

Segelman, A. B., Segelman, F., Karlinger, J., and Sofia, D. (1976). "Sassafras and Herb Tea. Potential Health Hazards." *Journal of the American Medical Association,* 236:477.
Siegel, R. K. (1976). "Herbal Intoxication." *Journal of the American Medical Association,* 236:473–476.
The Medical Letter Inc. (1979). "Toxic Reactions to Plant Products Sold in Health Food Stores." *Medical Letter,* 21:29–31.

Pesticides and Other Chemicals

American Farm Bureau Federation (1979). *Scientific Dispute Resolution Conference on 2,4,5–T.* American Farm Bureau Federation, Park Ridge, Illinois.
Brown, M. H. (1979). "Love Canal and What It Says About the Poisoning of America." *The Atlantic Monthly,* December, pp. 33–47.
C.D.C. (1977). *Insecticides for the Control of Insects of Public Health Importance.* U.S. Department of Health, Education, and Welfare, P.H.S. Center for Disease Control, Atlanta, Georgia 30333.
Clyne, R. M., and Shaffer, C. B. (no date). *Toxicological Information, Cyanamid Organophosphate Pesticides,* Third Edition. American Cyanamid Company, Agricultural Division, Princeton, N.J.
Cordle, F., Corneliussen, P., Jelinek, C., Hackley, B., Lehman, R., McLaughlin, J., Rhoden, R., and Shapiro, R. (1978). "Human Exposure to Polychlorinated Biphenyls and Polybrominated Biphenyls." *Environmental Health Perspectives,* 24:157–172.
Hall, R. H. (1974). *Food for Nought.* Harper and Row, New York.
Kolata, G. B. (1980). "Chromosome Damage: What It Is, What It Means." *Science,* 208:1240.
Kolata, G. B. (1980). "Love Canal: False Alarm Caused by Botched Study." *Science,* 208:1239–1241.

McEwen, F. L., and Stephenson, G. R. (1979). *The Use and Significance of Pesticides in the Environment*. John Wiley and Sons, New York, Toronto.

Stephenson, G. R. (1980). "2,4,5–T—Another Decade of controversy." *Dow Canadian Insight*, April, 3:11–13.

Winter, R. (1979). *Cancer-Causing Agents. A Preventive Guide*. Crown Publishers Inc., New York.

Food Poisoning and Parasites

Ager, E. A., et al (1967). "Two Outbreaks of Egg-borne Salmonellosis and Implications for Their Prevention." *Journal of the American Medical Association*, 199:372–378.

Aron, S. S., et al (1977). "Infant Botulism—Epidemiological, Clinical and Laboratory Aspects." *Journal of the American Medical Association*, 237:1946–1951.

Becker, C. E., et al (1976). "Diagnosis and Treatment of Amanita Phalloides–Type Mushroom Poisoning." *Western Journal of Medicine*, 125:100–109.

Benenson, A. (1975). *Control of Communicable Diseases in Man*, Twelfth Edition. American Public Health Association, Washington.

Black, R. E., et al (1978). "Epidemic *Yersinia Enterocolitica* Infection due to Contaminated Chocolate Milk." *New England Journal of Medicine*, 298:76–79.

Bryan, F. L. (1978). *Diseases Transmitted by Foods*. Center for Disease Control, Atlanta, Georgia. U.S. Department of Health, Education and Welfare, P.H.S. H.E.W. Publication No. (CDC) 78-8237.

Bryan, F. L. (1979). "Prevention of Foodborne Diseases in Food Service Establishments." *Journal of Environmental Health*, 41:198–206.

Center for Disease Control (1979). *Foodborne Disease Surveillance. Annual Summary 1978*. HEW Publication No. (CDC) 80-8185. U.S. Department of Health, Education and Welfare, P.H.S. Atlanta, Georgia.

Center for Disease Control (1979). *Botulism in The United States 1899–1977.* Handbook, U.S. Department of Health, Education and Welfare P.H.S. Atlanta, Georgia.

Dack, G. M., et al (1930). "An Outbreak of Food Poisoning Proved to be due to a Yellow Hemolytic Staphylococcus." *Journal of Preventive Medicine,* 4:167–175.

Fontane, R. E., et al (1978). "Raw Hamburger: An Interstate Common Source of Human Salmonellosis." *American Journal of Epidemiology,* 107:36–45.

Galli, C. L., Paoletti, R., and Vetlorazzi, G. (1978). *Chemical Toxicology of Food Elsevier/North Holland.* Biomedical Press, Amsterdam, New York, Oxford.

Hobbs, B. C., and Gilbert, R. J. (1978). *Food Poisoning and Food Hygiene,* Fourth Edition. Edward Arnold, London.

Last, J. M. (editor) (1980). *Public Health and Preventive Medicine,* Maxcy-Rosenau, Eleventh Edition. Appleton-Century-Crofts. New York.

le Riche, H., and Dunstan, T. (1953). "An Outbreak of Food Poisoning Amongst Nurses and Patients of the Pretoria Non-European Hospital." *South African Medical Journal,* 27:1102–1105.

Leers, W. D. (1973). "Salmonella Outbreak: A Case History. *University of Toronto Medical Journal,* 50:18–23.

Lerke, P. A., et al (1978). "Scrombroid Poisoning. Report of an Outbreak." *Western Journal of Medicine,* 129:381–386.

Riemann, H. (editor) (1969). *Food-Borne Infections and Intoxications.* Academic Press, New York, London.

Singal, M., et al (1976). "Trichinosis Acquired at Sea—Report of An Outbreak." *American Journal of Tropical Medicine and Hygiene,* 25:675–681.

Smith, H. W., and Crabb, W. E. (1961). "The Faecal Bacterial Flora of Animals and Man: Its Development in The Young." *Journal of Pathology and Bacteriology,* 82:53–66.

Steward, C. P., and Guthrie, D., (editors) (1963). *Lind's Treatise on Scurvy.* A bicentenary volume containing a reprint of the First edition by James Lind M.D. Edinburgh at the University Press.

Stone, E. M., et al (1971). "A Waterborne Epidemic of Salmonellosis in Riverside California, 1965. Epidemiologic Aspects." *American Journal of Epidemiology*, 93:33–48.

Taylor, J. (1960). *The Diarrhoeal Diseases in England and Wales*. Bulletin of the World Health Organization, 23:763–779.

Taylor, J. (1965). *Modern Life and Salmonellosis*. Proceedings of The Royal Society of Medicine, 58:167–170.

Taylor, J. (1965). "Salmonella Food Poisoning." *Practitioner*, 195:12–17.

Thomson, S. (1955). "The Numbers of Pathogenic Bacilli in Faeces in Intestinal Diseases." *Journal of Hygiene*, 53:217–224.

Trager, J. (1970). *Foodbook*. Grossman Publishers, New York.

Wilder, A. N., et al (1966). "Isolation of Salmonella from Poultry." *New England Journal of Medicine*, 274:1453–1460.

Data on Health and Disease

Brown, L. R. (1978). *The Twenty-Ninth Day*. A Worldwatch Institute Book. W. W. Norton and Company Inc., New York.

Canby, T. Y. (1980). "Our Most Precious Resource, Water." *National Geographic*, 158:144–179.

Goodhart, R. S., and Shils, M. E. (1973). *Modern Nutrition in Health and Disease*, Fifth Edition. Lea and Fibiger, Philadelphia.

International Asociation of Milk, Food and Environmental Sanitation Inc. (1979). *Procedures To Investigate Waterborne Illness*. P.O. Box 701, Aures, Iowa 50010.

Krause, M. V., and Mahan, L. K. (1980). *Food Nutrition and Diet Therapy*, Sixth Edition. W. B. Saunders Company, Philadelphia, London, Toronto.

Miller, A. P. (1962). *Water and Man's Health.* Department of State. Agency for International Development, Washington, D.C.

Office of Research and Development (1980). *Research Summary. Industrial Waste Water.* United States Environmental Protection Agency, Center for Environmental Research Information, U.S. EPA. Cincinnati, Ohio.

Ontario Ministry of the Environment (1978). *Water Management.* Water Resources Branch, Toronto.

Sekla, L., Stakiw, W., Kay, C., and VanBuckenhout, L. (1980). "Enteric Viruses in Renovated Water in Manitoba." *Canadian Journal of Microbiology,* 26:518–523.

Drugs in Pregnancy

American Farm Bureau Federation (1979). *Scientific Dispute Resolution Conference.* American Farm Bureau Federation, Park Ridge, Illinois.

Center for Disease Control (1979). "Temporal Trends in the Incidence of Morbidity and Mortality." Weekly Report, August 13, 28:401–402.

Clarren, S. K., and Smith, D. (1978). "The Fetal Alcohol Syndrome, 298:1063–1067.

Forfar, J., and Arneil, G. (1973). *Textbook of Paediatrics.* Churchill Livingstone, Edinburgh.

Goodwin, L. S., and Gilman, A. (1970). *The Pharmacological Basis of Therapeutics,* Fifth Edition. Macmillan, New York.

IARC Monograph (1978). *The Evaluation of the Carcinogenic Risk of Chemicals to Humans. Polychlorinated Biphenyls and Polybrominated Biphenyls.* International Agency for Research and Cancer Monographs on The Evaluation of the Carcinogenic Risk of Chemicals to Humans, 18:1–124 (1978).

Kolata, G. B. (1978). "Behavioural Teratology: Birth Defects of the Mind." *Science,* 202:732–734.

McEwen, F. L., and Stephenson, G. R. (1979). *The Use and Significance of Pesticides in the Environment*. John Wiley and Sons, New York, Toronto.

Streissguth, A. P., Landesman-Dwyer, S., Martin, J. C., Smith, D. (1980). "Teratogenic Effects of Alcohol in Humans and Laboratory Animals." *Science*, 209:353–361.

Surgeon General (1979). *Smoking and Health*. DHEW Publication No. (PHS) 79-50066, U.S. Department of Health, Education and Welfare, Public Health Service, Office on Smoking and Health.

Do Foods Cause Cancer?

Cairns, J. (1978). *Cancer Science and Society*. W. H. Freeman and Company, San Francisco.

Cummings, J. H. (1978). "Dietary Factors in the Aetiology of Gastrointestinal Cancer." *Journal of Human Nutrition*, 32:455–465.

Davies, J. W. (1975). *Cancer Patterns in Canada 1931–1974*. Bureau of Epidemiology, Laboratory Centre for Disease Control Health Protection Branch, Ottawa.

Davies, J. W. (1979). *Cancer Incidence Trends. Saskatchewan 1950–1975*. Bureau of Epidemiology, Laboratory Centre for Disease Control, Health Protection Branch, Ottawa.

Enig, M. G., Munn, R. J., and Keeney, M. (1978). "Dietary Fat and Cancer Trends—A Critique." Federation Proceedings, 37:2215–2220.

Enstrom, J. E. (1980). "Health and Dietary Practices and Cancer Mortality among California Mormons," from Cairns, J., et al (1980). pp. 69–92.

Gori, G. B. (1978). "Role of Diet and Nutrition in Cancer Cause Prevention and Treatment." *Bulletin Cancer*, 65:115–126.

Gori, G. B. (1979). "Dietary and Nutritional Implications in the Multifactorial Etiology of Certain Prevalent Human Cancers." *Cancer*, 43:2151–2161.

Lilienfeld, A. M. (1980). "Cancer, pp. 1147–1167, in Last, J. M. (editor) Maxcy-Rosenau, *Public Health and Preventive Medicine*. Eleventh Edition. Appleton-Century-Crofts, New York.

Lipsett, M. B. (1978). "Interaction of Drugs, Hormones and Nutrition in the Causes of Cancer." *Cancer*, 43:1967–1981.

Lipsett, M. B. (1979). "Interaction of Drugs, Hormones, and Nutrition in the Causes of Cancer." *Cancer*, 43:1967–1981.

Litven, W., Smith, H., and Wigle, D. T. (1980). "Recent Trends in Lung Cancer Mortality." *Canadian Lung Association Bulletin*, 59:4–5.

Lyon, J. L., Gardener, J. W., and West, D. W. (1980). "Cancer Risk and Life-Style: Cancer Among Mormons from 1967–1975," pp 3–30 from Cairns, J., Lyon, J. L., and Skolnick, M. (editors) 1980) *Banbury Report 4. Cancer Incidence in Defined Populations*. Cold Spring Harbor Laboratory. Banbury.

Maugh, T. H., II (1979). "Cancer and Environment: Higginson Speaks Out." *Science*, 205:163–

Miller, A. B., Kelly, A., Choi, N. W., Matthews, V., Morgan, R. W., Munan, L., Burch, J. D., Feather, J., Howe, G. R., and Jain, M. (1978). "A Study of Diet and Breast Cancer." *American Journal of Epidemiology*, 107:499–509.

Mortality Atlas of Canada (1980). Laboratory Centre for Disease Control, Health Protection Branch, Ottawa.

Newberne, P. M., and Suphakarn, V. (1977). "Preventive Role of Vitamin A in Colon Carcinogenesis in Rats. *Cancer*, 40:2553.

Oiso, T. (1975). "Incidence of Stomach Cancer and Its Relation to Dietary Habits and Nutrition in Japan Between 1900 and 1975." *Cancer Research*, 35:3254–3258.

Peters, J. A. (1975). "Summary of the Informal Discussion of the General Overview of Nutrition and Cancer." *Cancer Research*, 35:3301–3303.

Phillips, R. L., Kuzman, J. W., and Lotz, T. M. (1980). "Cancer Mortality Among Comparable Members versus Non-members of the Seventh Day Adventist Church," from Cairns, J., et al (1980), pp. 93–108.

Rawson, R. W. (1980). "The Total Environment in the Epidemiology of Neoplastic Disease: The Obvious Ain't Necessarily So," From Cairns, J., et al (1980), pp. 109–119.

Reddy, B. S. (1980). "Dietary Fibre and Colon Cancer: Epidemiologic and Experimental Evidence." *Canadian Medical Association Journal,* 123:850–856.

Schrauzer, G. N., and Ishmael, D. (1974). "Effects of Selenium and of Arsenic on the Genesis of Spontaneous Mammary Tumors in Inbred C3H Mice. Ann. Clin. Lab. Sci. 2:441.

Segi, M., and Kurihara, T. (1966). "Cancer Mortality for Selected Sites in 24 Countries, No. 4." (1962–1963). Department of Public Health, Tohoku University School of Medicine, Sendai, Japan.

Shamberger, R. J. (1970). "Relationship of Selenium to Cancer. I. Inhibitory effect of Selenium on Carcinogenesis." *Journal of the National Cancer Institute,* 44:931–.

Sorenson, A. (1980). "Methodology and Strategies for Nutritional Epidemiology. Studies Using a Diet and Colon Cancer Model," from Cairns, J., et al (1980), pp. 51–67.

Symposium American Cancer Society (1965). "Epidemiologic Approaches to Cancer Etiology." Reprinted from *Cancer Research,* 25:1271–1391.

Vitale, J. (1975). "Possible Role of Nutrients in Neoplasia." *Cancer Research,* 35:3320–3325.

Wattenberg, L. W., et al (1976). "Dietary Constituents Altering the Responses to Chemical Carcinogens." *Federal Proceedings,* 35:1327–

West, D. W. (1980). "An Assessment of Cancer Risk Factors in Latter-Day Saints and Non-Latter-Day Saints in Utah." From Cairns, J., et al (1980), pp. 31–49.

Wynder, E. L. (1979). "Dietary Habits and Cancer Epidemiology." *Cancer,* 43:1955–1961.

Atherosclerosis, Heart Disease, and Diet

Anderson, T. (1978). "A New View of Heart Disease." *New Scientist,* 77:374-376.

Anderson, T.W. (1979). "The Male Epidemic Heart Disease." *Public Health,* (London) 93:163-172.

Armstrong, M.L., Warner, E.D., and Connor, W.E. (1970). "Regression of Coronary Atheromatosis in Rhesus Monkeys." *Circulation Research,* 27:59-67.

Baker, L.W., and Houlder, A. (1973). "Deep Vein Thrombosis in Bantu and Indian Patients." *South African Medical Journal,* 47:1689-1692.

Barr, R.D., Ouna, N., and Kendall, A.G. (1973). "The Blood Coagulation and Fibrinolytic Systems in Healthy Adult Africans and Europeans—A Comparative Study." *Scottish Medical Journal,* 18:93-97.

Basta, L., Williams, C., Kioschos, J.M., and Spector, A.A. (1976). "Regression of Atherosclerotic Stenosing Lesions of the Renal Arteries and Spontaneous Cure of Systemic Hypertension Through Control of Hyperlipidemia." *The American Journal of Medicine,* 61:420-423.

Beighton, P., Solomon, L., Soskolne, C.L., and Sweet, B. (1972). "Serum Uric Acid Concentrations in a Rural Tswana Community in Southern Africa." *Annals of Rheumatic Diseases,* 32:346-350.

Benditt, E.P. (1979). "The Origin of Atherosclerosis." *Scientific American,* 236:74-85.

Berkowitz, D. (1964). "Blood Lipid and Uric Acid Interrelationships." *Journal of the American Medical Association.*

Burslem, J., Schonfeld, G., Howald, M.A., Weidman, S.W., Miller, J.P. (1978). "Plasma Apoprotein and Lipoprotein Lipid Levels in Vegetarians." *Metabolism,* 27:711-719.

Buskirk, E.R. (1977). "Diet and Athletic Performance." *Postgraduate Medicine,* 61:229-235.

Cooper, B., Stamler, J., Dyer, A., and Garside, D. (1978). "The Decline in Mortality from Coronary Heart Disease, U.S.A. 1968-1975." *Journal of Chronic Diseases,* 31:709-720.

Coronary Drug Project Research Group (1975). "Clofibrate and Niacin in Coronary Heart Disease." *Journal of the American*

Medical Association, 231:360-381.

Corrigan, J.J., and Marcus, F.I. (1974). "Coagulopathy Associated with Vitamin E Ingestion." *Journal of the American Medical Association,* 230:1300-1301.

Dick, T.B.S., and Stone, M.C. (1978). "Prevalence of Three Major Risk Factors in Random Sample of Men and Women, and in Patients with Ischaemic Heart Disease." *British Heart Journal,* 40:617-626.

Flynn, M.A., Nolph, G.B., Flynn, T., Kahrs, R., and Krause, G. (1979). "Effect of Dietary Egg on Human Serum Cholesterol and Triglycerides." *American Journal of Clinical Nutrition,* 32:1051-1057.

Glueck, C.J., and Connor, W. (1978). "Diet-Coronary Heart Disease Relationships Reconnoitred." *American Journal of Clinical Nutrition,* 31:727-737.

Kannel, W.B., and Sorlie, P. (1979). "Some Health Benefits of Physical Activity. The Framingham Study." *Archives of Internal Medicine,* 139:857-861.

Kavanagh, T. (1976). *Heart Attack? Counter-attack?* Van Nostrand Reinhold Ltd., Toronto.

Koletsky, S., and Snajdar, R. (1979). "Reduction of Vascular Disease in Genetically Obese Rats Treated for Hypertension and Hyperlipidemia." *Experimental and Molecular Pathology,* 30:409-419.

Leon, A.S., and Blackburn, H. (1977). "The Relationship of Physical Activity to Coronary Heart Disease and Life Expectancy." *Annals of the New York Academy of Science,* 301:561-578.

Malhotra, S.L. (1967). "Geographical Aspects of Acute Myocardial Infarction in India with Special Reference to Patterns of Diet and Eating." *British Heart Journal,* 29:337-343.

Mann, G.V. (1977). "Diet-Heart: End of an Era." *New England Journal of Medicine,* 297-644-650.

Marier, J.R., Neri, L., and Anderson, T.W. (1979). "Water Hardness, Human Health, and the Importance of Magnesium." NRCC No. 17581, National Research Council of Canada, Ottawa K1A OR6

McMichael, Sir John (1979). "Fats and Atheroma: An Inquest." *British Medical Journal,* 1:173-175.

Miller, N.E., Rao, S., Lewis, B., Bjorsuik, G., Myhre, K., and
    Mjos, O.D. (1979). "High-Density Lipoproteins and Physical
    Activity." *Lancet,* I: 111 (January 13).
Morris, J.N., Marr, J.W., and Clayton, D.G. (1977). "Diet and
    Heart: A Postscript." *British Medical Journal,* 2:1307-1314.
Morris, M.L., Fuller, V.M., Bruce, V.M., and MacDonald, B.E.
    (1977). "Absorption of Cholesterol from Eggs and the Effect on
    Serum Cholesterol Levels of Men." *Journal of the Canadian
    Dietetic Association,* 38:58.
Morrison, L.M. (1960). "Diet in Coronary Atherosclerosis."
    Journal of the American Medical Association, 173:104-108.
Noakes, T.D., and Opie, L.H. (1976). "The Cardiovascular Risks
    and Benefits of Exercise." *The Practitioner,* 216:288-296.
Porter, M.W., Yamanaka, W., Carlson, S., and Flynn, M.A.
    (1977). "Effect of Dietary Egg on Serum Cholesterol in
    Triglyceride of Human Males." *American Journal of Clinical
    Nutrition,* 30:490-495.
Report of a Joint Working Party of the Royal College of
    Physicians of London and The British Cardiac Society (1976).
    "Prevention of Coronary Heart Disease." *Journal of The
    Royal College of Physicians,* 10:213-275.
Sanders, T.A.B., Ellis, F.R., Dickerson, J.W.T. (1978). "Studies of
    Vegans: The fatty acid composition of plasma choline phos-
    phoglycerides, erythrocytes, adipose tissue, and breast milk,
    and some indicators of susceptibility to ischemic heart disease
    in vegans and omnivone controls." *American Journal of
    Clinical Nutrition,* 31:805-813.
Simons, L.A., Gibson, J.C., Paino, C., Hosking, M., Bullock, J.,
    and Trim, J. (1978). "The Influence of a Wide Range of
    Absorbed Cholesterol on Plasma Cholesterol Levels in Man."
    The American Journal of Clinical Nutrition. 31: 1334-1339.
Sirtori, C.R., Gianfranceschi, G., Gritti, I., Nappi, G., Brambilla,
    G., Paoletti, P. (1979). "Decreased High Density Lipoprotein-
    Cholesterol Levels in Male Patients with Transient Ischemic
    Attacks. *Atherosclerosis,* 32:205-211.
Slater, G., Mead, J., Dhopeshwarkar, G., Ribinson, S., and Alfin-
    Slater, R.B. (1976). "Plasma Cholesterol and Triglycerides in
    Men with Added Eggs in the Diet." *Nutrition Reports
    International,* 14:249-260.

The American Heart Association (1980). *Heartbook.* E.P. Dutton, New York.

Wade, N. (1980). "Food Board's Fat Report Hits Fire." *Science,* 209:248-250.

Williams, P., Robinson, D., Bailey, A. (1979). "High Density Lipoprotein and Coronary Risk Factors in Normal Men. *Lancet,* I:72-75.

Hypoglycemia, Hyperactivity, and Allergy

Feingold, B. F. (1975). *Why Your Child Is Hyperactive.* Random House, New York.

Holvey, D. N. (1972). *The Merck Manual,* Twelfth Edition. Merck & Co. Inc., Rahway, N.J.

Rowe, A. H., and Rowe, A. (1972). *Food Allergy.* Charles C. Thomas, Springfield, Illinois.

Walker, S. (1977). *Help for the Hyperactive Child.* Houghton Mifflin Company, Boston.

Williams, J. I., Cram, D. M., Tausig, F. T., and Webster, E. (1978). "Relative Effects of Drugs and Diet on Hyperactive Behaviours: An Experimental Study." *Pediatrics,* 61:811–817.

Wurtman, R. J., and Wurtman, J. J. (1979). *Nutrition and The Brain.* Raven Press, New York.

INDEX

holly, 68–69
hydrocarbons, chlorinated, 80
hyperactivity, 171–176
  causes of, 173–174
  diagnosis of, 176
  drugs in, 174–175
  and food additives, 175–176
  role of parent in, 173
hypertension, 160, 161
hypoglycemia, 167–171
  diagnosis of, 169
  diet for, 170–171
  symptoms of, 169
insecticides, toxicity testing of,
    81–85
  types of, 80–81
  see also *pesticides*
insulin, 167
ischemic heart disease, 156–159,
    161; see also *heart disease*
Japanese, calcium standards, 16
jimson weed, 66
kava kava tea, 65
laetrile, 31
lead poisoning, 55
LD$_{50}$, 84
  of household chemicals, 86
life expectation, 21, 155–156
Love Canal, 92, 121
malnutrition, U.S., 24–27
mercury contamination, 31, 55–56
metals, toxic, 54–56
methemoglobinemia, 123–124
milk, fortification of, 26
minimal brain dysfunction (MBD),
    171
Minimata disease, 56, 90
mistletoe, 69
mitral stenosis, 162
monosodium glutamate, 46–47
Mormons, 139–141
mortality, causes of, 154
mushrooms, poisonous, 69
mutagens, 78
  in atherosclerosis, 160

in pesticides, 90–91
narcotics, effects on fetus of, 128
natural poisons, 31–32
nitrates, nitrites, 34–35
  and stomach cancer, 147
  in water supply, 123–124
nitrosamines, 34–35
nutmeg, 45–46, 65
nutritional deficiency, 23–27
nutritional disease, 31
obesity, 27
oils, 13
organophosphates, 80
  poisoning by, 85
parasitic infections, 104
pellagra, 23
pesticides, 32, 75–92
  alternatives to, 79–80
  carcinogenicity of, 89–92
  importance of, 76–77
pheromones, 80
plants, poisonous, 68–69
poisons, natural, 59–76
pollution, water, 120–124
polybrominated biphenyls (PBBs),
    31, 88–89
polychlorinated biphenyls (PCBs),
    87–88
  in human milk, 129
polysorbate 60, 53
pregnancy, drugs in, 125–131
preservatives, 51–52
propyl gallate, 53
proteins, 11–12
  in common foods, 12
pyrethrin, 75
Red Dye 2, 44, 48
red tide, 70
rhubarb, 69
rickets, 13, 24
risks, comparative, 36–39
rotenone, 75
rubella, 126
saccharin, 33–34, 49
St. Anthony's Fire, 73